One for the
Girlos

ENYA MARTIN started her career in comedy making two-minute videos for her Facebook page 'Giz A Laugh'. She is now regarded as one of the best live stand-up comedians in Ireland and has sold out multiple shows in venues around the country. Her latest show is *Is it Just Me?*

Enya Martin

One for the Girlos

From the girls' night out to the group chat,
the ultimate survival guide

THE O'BRIEN PRESS
DUBLIN

Dedication

To my very own girlos – you know who you are! Thanks to everyone who has believed in me through this crazy journey so far: followers, fans, family and friends. I'm only getting started 😊!

First published in 2024 by
The O'Brien Press Ltd,
12 Terenure Road East, Rathgar, Dublin 6, D06 HD27, Ireland.
Tel: +353 1 4923333; Fax: +353 1 4922777
E-mail: books@obrien.ie
Website: obrien.ie

The O'Brien Press is a member of Publishing Ireland
ISBN: 978-1-78849-496-0
Text © copyright Enya Martin 2024
The moral rights of the author have been asserted
Copyright for typesetting, layout, editing, design
© The O'Brien Press Ltd

8 7 6 5 4 3 2 1
28 27 26 25 24

Cover design and internal design by Emma Byrne
Cover photo and author photo, p 2, by Sara Mcdonald
Internal illustrations throughout: Shutterstock.

Printed and bound by and bound by Nørhaven Paperback A/S, Denmark.

The paper in this book is produced using pulp from managed forests.

Published in

DUBLIN
UNESCO
City of Literature

Great Irish books
O'BRIEN
obrien.ie

MIX
Paper | Supporting
responsible forestry
FSC
www.fsc.org
FSC® C104608

Contents

Introduction   7

One: How Did I Become Friends with these People?   11

Two: Supporting Your Bestie Through a Break-up   35

Three: Work Friends are in a League of their Own   60

Four: Navigating the Female WhatsApp Group   84

Five: When the Girls' Holiday Makes it Out of the
    Group Chat   105

Six: Navigating a Girls' Night Out   143

Seven: Surviving a Hen Party   167

Eight: When Your Best Friend Becomes a Mother
    for the First Time   188

Nine: The First Friend to ...   216

In Conclusion ...   237

Introduction

Hi, I'm Enya Martin! A working-class Dub, born and bred in Clondalkin – gerrup, D22! You might know me as the online social media sensation 'Giz a laugh'. I've been making comedy skits online since 2014 – *way* before the TikTok kids! – back when you'd film things horizontally and edit the footage on Windows Movie Maker. I sound like a dinosaur, but I'm only thirty-one! Thankfully everything is on the aul' smartphones now; it all fits in your pocket.

I'm also a stand-up comedian. I progressed to stage in 2017, and have toured and performed in theatres and at comedy festivals all over Ireland. I've even sold out multiple nights in the Mecca of Irish comedy, Vicar Street. My dream of becoming a household name in Ireland by doing what I love most, making people laugh, is slowly becoming a reality. I'm a radio presenter on Dublin's FM104 and I'm also a personal trainer, yes … a personal trainer! I realise these professions are polar opposites; it's a bit like a UFC fighter opening up a garden centre.

As if I didn't have enough strings to my bow, now I can add 'author' to that list. So … welcome to my first book. Yes, that's right, the girl who got a D3 in Higher-Level English on the Leaving Cert. Thirteen years later, I finally figured out when I should or shouldn't use a comma. So why did I decide to write a book about female friendships? Why not a book about conquering the art of stand-up? Or how to go viral on Facebook, Instagram, and TikTok? How to grow your following, how to make a living from making content on social media?

Believe it or not, I studied Advertising and Marketing in college, I've got a degree in it. (Yep, people from council estates can progress to third-level education, too!) Why did I study Advertising and Marketing and not Acting or Drama? Well, my first option on the CAO form was creative digital media in IT Tallaght, Dublin. I wanted to explore the option of being on TV or radio. I always felt I had an outgoing personality (just ask my old classmates, I loved to poke fun at them and my teachers!), but never for a second did I contemplate stand-up. I just assumed I had to get a nine to five like everyone else. I enjoyed taking the piss out of friends and family, but I never thought I'd make a career out of it! Sadly, I didn't get into that creative digital media course, as I needed a C1 in Higher English on the Leaving Cert. (How do you not ace an exam in a language you're fluent in?) I ended up accepting my second option, Advertising and Marketing Communications. Business studies was one of my favourite subjects in secondary school. Why? I was fascinated with consumer behaviour. Which stems from my fascination with human behaviour in general.

Psychology was also one of my options in my CAO form. My mother always said I was like a sponge when I was a baby, I looked around at everyone and everything and soaked it all up. I loved to study how people spoke, behaved, acted. I would often do impressions of family members at dinner time to make my mam and dad laugh. That's what a comedian does, they study people, scenarios, life's trials and tribulations and make jokes out of it. People will only laugh at what they can relate to. When you're on stage and you're talking about the middle aisle in Aldi, everyone understands exactly what you're on about. So, when I posted my first funny sketch on Facebook, it had to be relatable, it had to be something people could look at and say, 'I know someone like that.' So I made a video about things I had a lot of experience in – being raised by an Irish mother, being in a relationship and so on. The content that always does well with my target audience, is content based around women and their friends and just how women behave in general. We're a complex species, I'm not denying that. Maybe your partner might benefit from this book too, who knows? The videos started to become popular really quickly, well at least judging by the comments:

'Omg, this is my mate!'

'Sarah, this is exactly how you go on!'

'I'd tag my friends, but they'll probably kill me!'

It appeared I wasn't the only woman who experienced these issues, scenarios and dilemmas with my friends. So instead of just using a video platform to get my comedy across on such a broad subject matter, I took it upon myself to write a book based on women and friendships, and how you can navigate all the classic scenarios: babies, hen parties, weddings, the workplace, girls' holidays, breakups ... or even if you just want to point at something and say 'Yep, that's me!' or 'That's my friend!'

Trust me, I've been studying these bitches since I was old enough to walk; think of this book as my survival guide! So sit back, grab a cup of tea or a glass of wine and jump into the world of female friendships!

CHAPTER 1

How Did I Become Friends with these People?

Friend (noun)

A person who will help you bury a body, no questions asked, no matter the time of day.

'Your honour, my friend did not have any involvement in the murder of my ex-husband; she did loan me her shovel, though.'

Similar: *Hun, Girlo, Slut, Bitch, Chick, Babes*

As kids we went through a lot of friends before we found a best friend. We had to experiment until eventually we found the ones that complemented our personality best. Friendships are a lot like relationships – you have to click, you have to be compatible, and they have to be able to take a slagging. Otherwise, they won't pass the vibe check.

When forming your first core group of friends as a child, you ignored the stuff that should really matter, like, 'Do these people add positive value to my life? Can I trust them? Can I rely on them?' As a kid, the only thing you cared about was, 'Does this person have the latest Barbie dream house, because my parents can't afford to buy me one, so I'll exploit Katie up the road and use her dream house until I get bored with it and just refuse point blank to go out and play with her from there on.' Friendship was built on a foundation of pure exploitation.

Sometimes that works out ok, though! A personal example is one of my best friends of twenty-five years; she became my bestie due to her father, Paddy, working in a biscuit factory. We were playing a game of chasing with all the kids on the road one summer's evening back in the year 1998 and it went something like this...

A man comes out to his front garden and calls his daughter's name.

PADDY

Sally!! Do your friends want a few biscuits?

SALLY

Would anyone like a few biscuits, me da
wants to know?

ENYA

I love biscuits! I'll have some.

I was the only child who took him up on his offer. I walked over
to the garden with his daughter and was greeted by a big box of
chocolate Kimberley biscuits.

PADDY

Now, love. Help yourself. Bring some
home to your ma if you want.

I thought to myself, *Get friendly with her, Enya, and you'll never
starve.* I'd knock into her house on the daily, not really giving a
shite if Sally was in or not, I just wanted the goods. And every day
without fail her dad would answer the door.

PADDY

She's up doing her homework, love. Do
you want to go up to her?

I walked into her room and lo and behold, a plate of Fig Rolls was upon her bed. *Jackpot.*

Sally would always insist we make beaded bracelets or play with our Baby Borns. No problem, Sally! Whatever I had to do to earn those biscuits was fine by me. I was always waiting for the next delivery. Biscuits on the way into the gaff and biscuits on the way out. My ma was always sorted for those unexpected visitors; our cupboards were bursting at the seams. One day, a few months into our friendship, one of the kids from the estate across the road robbed my Barbie clean out of my hands and ran away with it. I thought it was gone for good. I didn't know where they lived, I didn't stand a chance of getting it back. I was distraught, it was my favourite Barbie. Days later I was lying in bed, still grieving the loss of my beloved toy. Sally knocked on my front door. My mother called me downstairs, and I dragged myself from the room. There Sally was standing in my hall with my Barbie gripped to her chest.

SALLY

Here, I got your Barbie back. That dope across the road was out playing with it. I pushed her off her bike and it fell out of the front basket. So, I grabbed it and legged it. Here, me da sent in these to cheer you up.

A fresh box of chocky Kimbos! It was from that moment on I started taking our friendship a lot more seriously. Sally was actually all right. How many Fig Rolls would fight to get my toy back for me? That's right, none. Bickies will come and go, but a friend who would willingly risk getting grounded for your welfare, they're for life!

It was after that incident that I began to befriend people based on actual values. Would they have my back? Do they make me laugh? Are they a good influence on me? And all the materialistic stuff that came with them was just a bonus. Let's go through the types of friends we must all go through before forming a core group.

The Rich Friend

You befriended this person in school because they didn't live in your council estate; their parents owned their house. That was the first hint your friend's parents had money. 'Rich' did not necessarily mean they lived in a mansion and had an indoor pool; it meant their parents had a bigger disposable income and had jobs they'd probably gone to college to qualify for. For example, I had a friend who came from a well-to-do family. I would often go to their house after school for dinner. And the dinner was always top tier. You wouldn't get waffles, spaghetti hoops and fish fingers in this gaff. It was stir fries or a pasta dish, and fresh fruit to snack on. All their cutlery matched (unlike my mother's collection of miscellaneous utensils collected over the years.) Katie had a massive trampoline out her back garden that was built into the ground and her parents had two cars and could afford Sky digital, meaning they had the Disney channel.

KATIE

Did you watch Lizzie McGuire last night?

ENYA

No, I don't have the Disney Channel, so I just watched the Six One news.

KATIE

What's that? Is that on Nickelodeon?

Back in the 90s or early 00s if you had a downstairs toilet or double-glazed windows you must have had money to burn! The first time I had dinner at Katie's house, I got home and my mother aggressively interrogated me about everything. The kitchen was like a casino, she went through that many cigarettes with the stress.

ENYA

When I asked if I could use the toilet upstairs, she said there was one down the hall that I could use. But I misheard her when she said it was the door on the left, and I opened the one on the right and I went into the wrong room. It had a washing machine in it and a dryer.

MA

OMG a utility room, I thought they were a myth! Probably has a mobile down the country too, the bitch!

ENYA

She does! I'm going next week; they invited me for the Easter weekend.

MA

Oh, for fuck's sake, I'll have to send you down in the best of gear and skip me ESB bill to give you enough spending money. Wouldn't want them talking about me.

ENYA

The ma is actually really nice, she gave me a scented candle to give to you.

MA

Does she think I can't afford my own candles? Probably an unwanted Christmas gift. 'Oh, we'll give that to the pauper family'. Might come in use, though, when my elecky gets cut next weekend.

The Bad Influence Friend

Mixing and experimenting with kids around the area was part of growing up. Finding those friends who suited you most. But there was also a lot of trial and error. Friends who *you* thought were good for you, but your mother was old enough and wise enough to know no good would come from being friends with Mad Becky around the corner. Becky's house was the only one on the road with no central heating, and boarded-up windows. They'd been put through so many times, I don't think her mother wanted to waste her money fixing them anymore. My mother would always tell me the PG version of what Becky's family was known for and to stay well away or I'll end up just like her. She'd constantly repeat that old saying to me, anytime she'd catch me with Becky, 'Show me your company and I'll tell you what you are.' Becky and I ended up becoming pals through a mutual friend. Becky gave me my first smoke at the age of twelve, and I coughed up a lung.

'You'll be grand, everyone is like that after their first!' she said. 'No, they're not for me.' I replied.

She was the first friend to bring me on a bus into Dublin city centre without parental guidance at the age of ten. I felt like Kevin McCallister lost in New York. All I had was my bus fare, so I spent the whole day window shopping. My mother was worried sick.

Becky was mad for carnivals too, anytime a carnival came to town she'd be begging me to go on these extreme rides that I was barely tall enough to get on. You know those rides where a fella who is, without question, an ex-convict spins you around on the waltzers like it's the wheel of fortune, 'SCREAM IF YOU WANNA GO FASTAA!' Becky tried multiple times to get me to go on the mitch from school. But unlike her, I valued my life and didn't want to face the wrath of my Irish mother. Becky was the only friend who ever got me grounded. We drifted apart as we grew older when I went into secondary school and met friends who weren't adrenaline junkies.

The Friend Who Always got Sick at Sleepovers

Childhood sleepovers were the equivalent of a night on the tiles when you're an adult. You didn't have to go home and sit by yourself in your room. You were surrounded by your mates having the craic and getting up to mischief. The sleepover would have been planned weeks in advance. It's all you would talk about in the days leading up. What movies you would watch. What PJs you would wear, what goodies you were going to eat. The innocence of it all. Not a penny from our own pocket either. The best sleepovers were the ones you didn't plan. When you and your mate were having such a good time in their room playing games and having a laugh, but it was 8pm in the evening and you knew home time was looming.

LILY

My ma said you've to go home soon.

ENYA

Ah really, can we not wait until the end of this game?

LILY

Why don't you stay over?

ENYA

Oh really?

LILY

Yeah, but I'm not asking my ma, you ask her, she won't say no if you ask her.

ENYA

Oh no, I'm not asking her. She's your ma!

LILY

She'll say no to me, but she won't say no
to you! Go on, just go down and ask her.

ENYA

Ugh. What will I say?

LILY

Just say 'Heya Catherine, I was wondering if I could stay over tonight so me and
Lily can finish playing our game.

ENYA

I'm shitting.

LILY

You'll be grand, I'll wait upstairs.

The walk down the stairs is what I imagine it feels like for Tyson
Fury walking into a sold-out MGM arena. I was petrified. I
walked into the kitchen where I found her mother cleaning the
dishes and utensils from the dinner. (Pork chops and spuds #rank.

Where's Paddy with the chocky Kimbos when you need him?)

It wasn't a coincidence that she was drying a carving knife.

ENYA

Heya, Catherine. Lily wants to know if it's alright that I stay tonight so we can finish playing our game.

('For god's sake!!' I hear faintly from the top of the stairs.)

CATHERINE

Oh, did she ask you to ask me, did she? Why does that not surprise me? Lily has to be up early to go to her nanny's, so unfortunately not tonight, Enya. And after the last time, I don't fancy getting up at 2am to bring you home.

Ouch. Now let's talk about the friend who gets sick at every sleepover. I was that child. And if you were too, we weren't sick, it was the onset stages of generalized anxiety disorder. I would always love the idea of a sleepover, but it was when the lights went off and I realized I was on my own, that's when I became a whinge bag. I missed the comfort of my own bed, and the security of my own room, and the familiarity of my own home. What if I got a bad spell of diarrhoea and had to flush the friend's toilet several times at three in the morning? These were the type of things that would run through my head as I lay in their bed, shaking about the unknown of the next eight hours. Everything would start out great. My friend's mother would pop her head in at around 10pm while we were painting our nails.

CATHERINE

I'm off to bed girls, ok? Just keep the noise down, if you want any snacks or drinks, there's loads down in the press. Just don't stay up too late.

LILY

Ok, we won't, ma.

ENYA

Thanks, Catherine.

CATHERINE

Goodnight.

As soon as that door would close, reality would hit hard. *Oh no, how will I get home if I don't feel well later? What if there's an alarm set? No, you'll be grand Enya just give it another couple of hours.* Before you know it, the lights are gone off and it's just you and your thoughts. It would go a bit too quiet, so you'd break the silence.

ENYA

I don't feel well.

LILY

What? You'll be grand just try and go asleep. I'll get you some flat 7Up if you get sick.

ENYA

No. I want to go home. I miss me ma.

LILY

Your ma lives four doors down. How do you miss her?

ENYA

I think I'm going to get sick.

At this stage her mother bursts

through the door and turns the light on,

still half asleep.

CATHERINE

What's all the racket? It's 2am, Lily, why
aren't you both asleep?

LILY

Enya doesn't feel well, and she wants to
go home.

CATHERINE

Home? Your ma will be fast asleep, Hun.
You'll have to wait until the morning.

At this point the chances of getting back to my own bed are slim
to none. So, I just go for the jugular and start crying uncontrolla-
bly and hope for the best.

ENYA

I need to get sick.

LILY

OMG!

CATHERINE

Oh ffs. Let me get my coat. Your mother is going to go through me, banging down her door at this time. She won't be staying over anymore after this; do you hear me, Lily!!

Thankfully I've grown out of it, because at this age, wherever I lay down, no matter where in the world, and get five minutes to myself, that's my home and that's good enough for me.

Your first gay best friend

This one is interesting because when you were a child you were very innocent and ignorant about sexuality, so you would just assume your friend Jamie from your road, who also likes Barbies and Britney, was just really fun to be around and understood you and your girlfriends more than any other boy. And he was just so much funnier and had a way with words, a razor-sharp tongue and a comeback for everything. He would hold workshops in his front garden and teach you how to dance like Christina Aguilera, walk in heels like a Victoria's Secret model or blend your pound-shop eye shadow with the correct technique. Sometimes during summer holidays, we would put on plays for our parents, Jamie was a Moore Street trader and we were his competitors.

JAMIE

Four bananets for a Euroooo!! Last of the bananets!

You would always think *something* was different, but you couldn't quite put your finger on it until you both grew up a bit and he started fancying the same boys as you. Ah, so *that's* what it was. Every girl needs a gay best friend, who else is going to tell you, 'That dress doesn't do any favours for your figure, hun!' while the rest of your mates blow smoke up your arse.

I also had a friend called Katie in primary school. She was light years ahead of us all, very mature, wasn't into bitchiness or gossiping, very strong-headed, great to have around during emergencies.

'Ah here. it's only a daddy-long-legs, give it to me. I'll get rid of it. Shite bags, the lot of yas!'

The lads were terrified of her. She took no shit from anyone; Katie was the girl you wanted around to defend you when the bullies came lurking. While we all chased boys around the school yard looking for a kiss, Katie was down the other end of the yard trying to get a game of football with the lads in the years above us. I thought she just liked looking at them in their O'Neill's shorts. But while we were pinning posters of Westlife on our bedroom walls, she was pinning posters of Queen Latifah and Missy Elliot on hers.

27

My mother loved her. Katie could do no wrong in her eyes; we had her over for dinner one day after school and my mother didn't shut up about her for the rest of the school year.

'How's that Katie girl? The one that plays the football? She's lovely, you should bring her around more often, she loves my cooking!'

I noticed as I got older and became more obsessed with boys and having a fella, Katie didn't share that same desire. She became really close with a girl, Jessica, off her football team. They were inseparable, for years you wouldn't see one without the other. I started to think, *Is Katie … gay?*

Turns out, she was, and she married aul Jessica. While my other school friends are doing the school run Monday to Friday, and don't have time to piss, Katie and Jess are off cruising another continent somewhere in the world.

Having friends like Jamie and Katie just proves that your sexuality and ability to be a good friend aren't mutually exclusive. I don't care if you've a tail coming out of your arse and two horns on your head, if I can trust you, rely on you, have the craic with you, and bury a body with your help, no questions asked. You can marry or ride who you want.

The Friend with Really Strict Parents

Did anyone else have someone they claim was their best friend, but you never saw them because they were grounded for most of their childhood? You spent more time waving at them through their bedroom window than you did playing with them.

I had one of those friends. Her name was Donna. She was never allowed to get dirty during grass fights. Couldn't get wet during water fights. Wasn't allowed out to play if it was cloudy, as there was a chance it would rain and then her clothes would be wet. She wasn't allowed to play outside in her school uniform. Wasn't allowed to leave the road. The list was endless. Those types of friends ended up rebelling the most out of all your friends, in their teenage years. What is that old saying? Strict parents create sneaky teenagers. She became the type of friend that would come up with the best alibis. She would tell her mother she was at a sleepover with a friend and then leave the house in her PJs with a school bag full to the brim with alcopop bottles.

STRICT MOTHER
Where are you going?

DONNA
I'm just going around to Enya's; we're having a sleepover.

STRICT MOTHER

I hope you're not drinking again? The
last time that happened you were so violently sick it was like someone shoved a
power hose up your arse!

DONNA

No, I swear I'm not, I wouldn't put myself
through that again. I promise I learned
my lesson.

*Continues to make a beeline toward the
front door. Glass bottles rattling in the process.*

STRICT MOTHER

What's that noise? Are there glass bottles
in your bag!? Is it alcohol!?

*Cue the Jaws theme. Think Donna,
THINK!!*

DONNA

No, of course not, me and Enya are getting a head start on our homework. We have to do a recycling project.

The mother studies Donna suspiciously

STRICT MOTHER

A recycling project? Well, aren't you very good at doing your homework on the weekend! I was blessed with a good child while there's other kids out there smoking hash and drinking cider in the fields behind their parents' backs.

DONNA

I know. Shame on them! I'll see you tomorrow!

The Compulsive Liar Friend

In adulthood these types of friends still exist, but you're not as gullible. As a child, you'd swallow a brick.

My friend Carly has been to Eleven-rife if you've been to Tenerife. If you got ten Easter eggs she got twenty. If your dad was a fireman, her da was the second man on the moon. If you got one Valentine's Day card from a secret admirer, she got ten.

31

I'll always remember the day she came into school after Pancake Tuesday and said she ate fifty pancakes. I went home that day to try to beat her record and nearly overdosed on pancake batter, almost killing myself in the process.

If I could turn back time, I should have just challenged Miss Liabetes there and then.

'Bring in the ten Valentine's Day cards, and prove it, ya big waffler!'

These friends grow up to portray the perfect life and relationship on social media, but behind closed doors they're probably living a Champagne lifestyle on a lemonade wage, and their fellas, who are made out to be Prince Charmings, are serial cheaters.

The Friend on your Nanny's Road

If your nanny lived over the other side of the city, you obviously couldn't bring your friends with you when you went to visit. So you'd either sit in her house all day, watching John Wayne westerns, being force-fed Madeira cake (not a Fig Roll to be seen), and that got boring really quick. Or, once you were allowed to play outside on the road unsupervised, you'd soon pluck up the courage to venture outside her garden and see what would come of it.

I had just one friend on my nanny's road. We were ten years old, and we bonded over our love of skipping ropes. This girl had my poor nanny's head melted. She would always forget my name, so she would knock on my grandparents' front door on a Monday and just say, 'Is the girl there?' I imagine this is how the Grim Reaper appears at the family home, when one's time on earth is up.

'No,' my nanny would tell her, 'she only comes over on Saturdays. How many times do I have to tell you?'

She would proceed to still knock in on Tuesday, Wednesday, Thursday and Friday for the years to follow. When my nanny passed away, that was the end of that.

A few years back, she added me on Facebook, asking me to promote her cake business: 'Are you that girl whose nanny lived on my road? Jesus, how's things? Any chance you want a free sponge, if you give me page share, Hun?'

There is one non-negotiable that I think all relationships should be built on – a shared sense of humour. I don't care if you're rich, gay, afraid of your mother, vomit at sleepovers, tell the odd white lie – humour trumps all! If you can't make me laugh at my own mother's funeral, don't waste my time. If you're not in a nursing home with me at the age of ninety showing me memes about haemorrhoids, thanks, but no thanks. If you don't absolutely roast me on my wedding day in front of my in-laws, then no I don't want to go out to play with you.

Some friendships fade with age while others stand the test of time, but regardless of their duration, they'll all help shape us in some way and teach us what we do want and what we don't want in an eternal friendly companion. So, here's to the kids that never fully qualified for the best friend role, the ones who smoked, lied about pancakes, and didn't stock Fig Rolls in their kitchen cupboard. May their spirits forever linger in our hearts, reminding us of the trials and tribulations of those formative years. And here's to the friends we're still yet to meet.

CHAPTER 2

Supporting Your Bestie Through a Break-Up

So, remember in childhood when you met your first best friend? You go through your first school trip together, first Halloween together, first Communion together, first Confirmation together, first period together, first teenage disco together. And then comes the first relationship, which you won't experience together, because that would be eh, a bit weird. Or so your boyfriend would think. Men think they are in a relationship with just one woman, but they're unaware they are actually in a relationship with all of her friends, or at least her nearest and dearest. I like to call this group of friends the 'board of directors'. Everything is discussed in great detail: icks, sex life, *size*, skills in the bedroom, bad habits, good habits, red flags, green flags. Men don't have a say in it because they won't be told about it, *ever*. Men on the other hand don't really disclose that much information with their friends about their relationship, or so I've heard. Which is understandable because women are perfect, aren't we?

However, the first relationship you enter can cause a rift between best friends, as you now experience someone else sharing your bestie. Your bestie may not have as much free time anymore, no last-minute trips to the shopping centre for a quick look, because she's on a hike up a mountain somewhere with him, when you only ever knew her as a lazy bitch who detested exercise. Drinks on a Saturday night become rare because she's cuddled up with him in her bed doing Netflix and chill and whatever else. The bed *you* used to share not so long ago to watch Disney movies! They become less responsive via WhatsApp because they're on Facetime with him.

Jealousy starts to creep in. Even if this man is perfect for your friend, you can't help but envy the prick, just a little. You're a lone ranger now.

When you *do* get to see your bestie you spend the whole time talking about him.

'Oh, Anto does this!'

'Oh, wait till I tell you what Anto said.'

'Oh, Anto brought me here, there, everywhere.'

'Soz, galz! Can't go, I'm helping Anto with something.'

'Wait till I show you what Anto bought me!'

Ah, Anto, me hole!! I want my friend to be happy, but at the same time, will he just be an arsehole, so I can have my bestie to myself again? However, be careful what you wish for ladies, there's a happy medium, you'll either have a friend who finds her Prince Charming straight away or else has terrible luck and always ends up with a prick, in and out of relationships more times than Take That have got back together. In that case you don't have much to worry about because you know she'll return to the nest soon enough, because she loves a good red flag.

Let's discuss the friends in every group and their issues with men:

The friend who met a boy when she was sixteen and stayed with him forever.

We will call her 'Michelle'. *Je ma pel, Michelle.* Junior Cert Spanish rearing its head there, or is that French? No, definitely Italian.

Michelle always went for the boys with green flags, kissed one or two frogs, but ultimately ended up with her Prince Charming very early on, her childhood sweetheart. Kissed in the park one Saturday night back in her teens, under the influence of a few alcopops. He became the reason she had her father's heart broke, constantly topping up her phone with free Meteor texts. They were each other's other halves on Bebo, which was a huge step in your relationship back then! Shared their love on Bebo every day; do you remember the three hearts? You had to give them out cautiously, if you were giving them all to the one boy, he *must* have been special.

They sat their Junior Cert together, Leaving Cert, went to each other's Debs, had their first holiday together. Maybe they went to separate colleges, but they still stood the test, experienced their first real jobs together, rented their first apartment together, bought their first home. He put a ring on it and they became first-time parents together.

At first you disliked him because he was moving in on your friendship territory. But he's been around that long, he's like one of the girls at this stage. It eventually became very hard to dislike him. Even if he did act prickish the odd time, he managed to always redeem himself. Every girl wants her friend to end up with someone like this. Sometimes they're almost too good to be true. Is there something she never told us about him? Maybe he claps when the plane lands? Does he have three nipples? No, because you all holidayed together one year, and you only spotted two. Is he shit in bed? Nah, there's no way she'd have stayed this long with him if he never ventured outside missionary. Maybe he has holes in his jocks? Maybe he takes the gherkins off of hamburgers in McDonalds? Whatever it is, he can't be perfect.

 ### The friend who never has any luck in love.

We'll call her Jessica. God love Jessica. She's like a lighthouse for a red flag. She loves a bad boy. You only have to see his photo to know he's bad news. Usually, it's a dead giveaway when you see his occupation on social media, listed as 'Full-time mad bastard'. She's only ever kissed frogs; Prince Charming doesn't appeal to her – too boring, he has to have daddy issues, and was probably never hugged as a child. These friends grow up to be part of multiple love triangles. Meaning, she'll end up as a mistress once or twice unbeknownst to her because she falls for love-bombing every time.

'Ah, girls he told me I'm the best thing that ever happened to him, he's never felt this way before about anyone, I think this fella might be the one.'

And all her friends are like, 'He probably told his *current* wife that bullshit too, hun.' It's hard to keep up with her because she goes through so many short-term relationships, you don't know what lad she's got on the go this week or next. She has had that many short-term relationships, she eventually starts coming across lads with the same name. She'll have them listed on her phone as, **John with the nose, John with two kids, John with the abs.**

 The friend who gets the ick about literally anything and will more than likely end up alone because she's so picky.

We will call her Martina. At least Jessica will settle for just about anyone he buys her a Louis Vuitton handbag and a pair of Gucci sunglasses.

CIARA

Martina, are you still with that lad who calls his ma, 'mummy'?

MARTINA

Ah no, he's long gone girls, I got the ick when I saw him hold his nose jumping into the pool on holidays.

NICOLA

He was lovely, Martina; he worshiped the ground you walked on! Remember that fella Mick who always sent you flowers on a Friday?

MARTINA

Yeah, he was nice until I saw how he walked down a hill. It was like he was walking in italics.

NICOLA

Or that lad who always brought your ma for lunch on a Sunday.

MARTINA

Oh, James? Lovely chap until I saw him run for a bus. Ick!

CIARA

Or that fella who would always drop us home after a night out and wait until we got through the front door to drive off.

MARTINA

That was Carl, his breathing annoyed me. Can you not breathe subtly like everyone else? Or maybe not breathe at all?

CIARA

Or the one who got a hotel room, covered the whole place in rose petals and love-heart balloons and asked you to be his girlfriend. Very romantic. He was near perfect, what was wrong with him again? He was hard to beat.

MARTINA

It just gave me the ick how he held his knife and fork. I just couldn't bear it anymore. Can you not hold them like a human being? I lasted longer than usual with him.

NICOLA

Ah, Martina, you're far too picky! That fella Paddy you were seeing for a while, and we were all mad about him as well, always brought you on holiday, wanted kids with you, the lot!

MARTINA

Omg, did you not notice how he drank a pint? His eyes would always move side to side. Ick!

CIARA

Remember you broke up with the lad from your gym because of the bank he was with?

MARTINA

Oh God, I couldn't bear the orange bit on the card!

This type of friend will grow old with no children nor significant other and have the audacity to say to their friends, 'Why does nobody want me? Will I die alone?'

Well, Martina, maybe if you weren't so fucking picky, you'd have the gaff with the white picket fence and a school of children to take care of you. Maybe don't be so judgemental the next time you see a man with a Velcro wallet or who has a few cats.

The friend who forgets you exist once they get back into their toxic relationship.

These girls will be at your beck and call in between relationships, will always be the first to arrange nights out, cinema dates, girls' holidays, but once a man comes along they forget who was there for them through all the drama, the heartbreak, the late night phone calls. When their toxic ex gets their claws back into them and they accept his half arsed apology, the cycle starts again and they slip off into the abyss. They've fallen off the face of the earth. Anytime you suggest a mate date, they're suddenly ill, or they're up to their eyes with work. If ever there was an ick with friends, this is it.

Red Flags that you Forget your Friends when in a Relationship.

1. You forget to post the annual birthday Instagram photo collage of all your crazy memories together. A declaration of love to your bestie, with Stevie Wonder's rendition of Happy Birthday playing over it. These photos consist of drunken nights out, hungover mornings, special occasions, and the noughties throwbacks when winged eyeliner and leopard print tops were all the rage.

2. You are radio silent in the WhatsApp group. Every message is given two blue ticks, but never a response. Your friends

become really suspicious of your ignorance when it comes to planning one of their birthdays, or a meet up. Or when they're looking for advice, or need help with something, yours is the only response absent from the group. You're convinced that if you don't reply for long enough, they won't notice anymore. Incorrect, it only magnifies your absence. Especially when you were the main meme contributor back before the man came on the scene.

3. Cancel plans at the last minute. You soon realize your absence in the WhatsApp group isn't going unnoticed, so you make a conscious effort to text a response every so often or give the thumbs up and agree to meet up for the monthly lunch or wine nights. However, you are well aware you have no intention of going, but you wait until the final hour to pull out. You've had every illness under the sun; it's like you open up the medical dictionary and look up what you haven't had yet. Everyone is waiting for the inevitable text on the day:

'Hey ladies, I know we were supposed to do Kris Kindle tonight at Martina's, but me ma must have undercooked the vegan sausages at dinner because I'm vomiting rings around myself! Sorry to cancel at the last minute. We will defo have to catch up soon and I can give my person their present. Enjoy!'

This friend is most certainly not suffering from vegan food poisoning, she's sitting in her fella's sitting room watching him play *Call of Duty*, afraid she'll miss something!

4. Only make plans when your boyfriend is away. Oh, so *now* you suddenly want to go to Penney's with your mates or go for a coffee because he's away on a stag do or with his kids for the weekend or in work? You think your friends don't notice you slip in and out whenever he's unavailable, but they do notice. They are also friends with him on social media and start to put two and two together. 'Isn't it convenient that you only ever hear from Mary when he's with his kids or his mates?' Don't be that friend!

5. You aren't there for them when they need you. The number-one attribute of a good friend is being there when your friend is at their lowest. Nothing should get in the way, bar their kids (eye roll). It's a bit shitty when your friend has been there for you whenever you've had murder with the boyfriend, no matter the time, day or night, but once the tables turn, you're nowhere to be seen. This is a major red flag in a friendship – it's so one sided.

The friend who portrays the perfect relationship on social media.

We all have one in the group, don't we? The sun shines from

his arse and he can do no wrong. Every woman following them on Instagram wonders when *their* knight in shining armour is going to come along and sweep them off their feet, like this fella allegedly does. He comes across as so impressive on social media that it actually causes rifts in other relationships. Particularly on the woman's end. 'Now, look at this fella constantly bringing his girlfriend away and showering her with flowers and chocolates on a weekly basis? Why can't you be like that instead of scratching your arse?' When in reality it's probably these women who already have their knight in shining armour; their love doesn't need to be *bought* nor does their relationship need validation. It's usually the friend that has the most to brag about, that hides the most.

> 'Omg woke up to these amazing flowers from himself, isn't he just the cutest?'

Translation: He forgot the date of our anniversary last week because he was out watching football all day and night and turned his phone off and we missed our reservation at the restaurant.

> 'My boyfriend is better than yours! When you think you're going on a staycation, you get into his car, he tells you you're going to need your

passport because you won't get to Disneyland without it! Luckiest girl alive right now.'

Translation: You *knew* you were going to Disneyland all along, because if he brought you to Westport for your birthday, it wouldn't impress your followers enough to like your post and you thrive off validation.

> *'Was having a really tough week and he comes through the door with a brand-new Marc Jacobs tote bag from Brown Thomas. He's the sweetest soul.'*

Translation: You discovered he's been liking other girls' pictures on social media and is trying to buy your forgiveness for how sleazy he is.

 The friend who doesn't want a relationship, just friends with benefits or a monthly/drunk hook up as she's too career driven.

Some of our friends are quite happy to be alone; they thrive like this. They look at their friends that are years deep into a relationship, are joined at the hip and must do everything together, holiday together, eat together, shit together. This friend couldn't imagine anything worse. (Alexa play 'Independent Women' by Destiny's Child). Her occasional dial-a-ride is enough to keep her sexual appetite alive. She'd love nothing more than to be the drunk aunt at the kids' parties, and have holidays two or three times a year, one of which would be a cruise. And if by chance she *does* marry one day, it will be to a man who is extremely wealthy, who will die under mysterious circumstances, and she will inherit all his money.

One thing all these types of friends have in common, is that at some stage they will probably go through a break-up. So... How do you support your friend through a break-up?

Here are my top tips:

Although our friends will experience many ups and downs with relationships throughout our friendship together, supporting them through a break-up is what separates a part-time friend from a bestie. Who is their go-to person whenever they have issues with their significant other? That's when you know they really value your opinion. Although you might give the WhatsApp group a brief lowdown on your situation, if you don't have a separate group chat with your bestie with the in-depth details of your break-up, do you even have a bestie? For the record, an *official* break-up isn't telling your friends you're done with him because you stayed in your ma's gaff for one night and blocked him on WhatsApp app when you've only been seeing each other a wet day. Let's talk about those long-term relationships in which you experienced many milestones together and you both decide to part ways once and for all.

What qualifies as an *official* break up?

1. All pictures of you and him on Instagram are deleted.
2. You unfollow each other on all social media platforms and WhatsApp. Strong believer in the no contact rule!
3. The cryptic self-love quotes start to emerge on your Instagram stories and Facebook timeline.

> **"**
>
> It's better to be **single with a standard** than losing yourself for approval'.

> Don't cry
> because it's over,
>
> *smile*
>
> because it's someone
> else's problem.

4. You move all your stuff back to your parents' house and return to your childhood bedroom until you can find alternative accommodation.

5. You're both back on dating apps. There's no going back from there.

6. And in extreme cases, the wedding is called off. #Raging #Snapping

If you are the chosen one that your bestie confides in about the deep stuff, here are the dos and don'ts when supporting them through the heartbreak of a breakup.

Don't

• Give your crazy friend the full lowdown about said bestie's break up, especially if it ended badly. She will find a weapon of choice (most likely a hammer of some sort), and take pleasure in smashing up the lad's work van. Getting violent or aggressive has never solved anything. (Unless you get clamped on a side street, 'Eh there's no clear sign to say it was a loading bay! Dope!')

- Don't force her back out into the dating world or push her onto some random bloke in a bar too soon after the breakup.

Martina

Nicola, get stuck into him over there, he's been eyeing you up all night! Tall, dark and ginger, right up your street.

Nicola

The telly is above my head and the match is on, that's why he's been looking over at me all night and he's wearing a wedding ring!?

Martina

Just because you're on a diet doesn't mean you can't look at the dessert menu.

- Don't keep updating your friend about her ex's social media posts or whereabouts.

Martina

Seen that prick out the other night on his Instagram stories. Loads of girls flocking around him. One of them had a big fuck-off tattoo on her arm of a cat. I don't know what's worse, her tattoo or him wearing skinny jeans with the rips in them.

Nicola

That sounds like his sister.

Martina

Just as well you're away from him, interbreeding with his sister. That's a mad family altogether.

- Don't tell her what you really thought of him. There's still be a very slim chance she'll get back together with him and if you've been badmouthing him, she's less likely to share the news with you.

Nicola

Me and James are separated, I'm staying in the apartment, and he's moved all his stuff back into his mams. It's been a long time coming but it's the best solution because I know my worth and he doesn't.

Ciara

So sorry to hear Hun, I'm here for you whenever you need me. Or even just to vent.

Martina

Don't poxy mind him, that rotten looking Ron Weasley yoke would be lucky to find half the woman you are. And the smell of body odour off him, did he ever shower, Nicola? Like, I know we all sweat a bit with work and that, but this wasn't normal. And please someone get him on a plane to Turkey ASAP and sort those teeth out. Is that why he never smiled in pictures? Or was he always a miserable fuck? And he's a shite electrician too, ever since he fixed my bathroom light, anytime I flush the toilet, it's like I'm at a rave because it turns into a bleedin' strobe light.

Ciara

Jesus, Martina.

Martina

What? She's not with him anymore.

Dos:

- Be supportive on social media. When your friend is going through her heartbreak quotes stage on Facebook, be their biggest cheerleader.

> 66
>
> **It's better to be single with a standard** than losing yourself for approval'.

Comments
- *Say it again for the people in the back!*

> Don't cry because it's over,
>
> *smile*
>
> because it's someone else's problem.

Comments
- *100 per cent, and all I'll say is God love her, whoever she is....*

- Be the meme queen. There can never be enough funny memes sent into a WhatsApp group about an ex-boyfriend. Humour is the best medicine.
- Whatever it takes to let her get it all off her chest. Perhaps a wine night with you or other friends? Sometimes our friends can keep their cards close to their chest because they're afraid of being a burden to us. A drunken mind speaks a sober heart.

NICOLA

I knew it was doomed from a few months ago. We were constantly arguing.

A bottle of wine deep into conversation.

MARTINA

We didn't have a clue what was going on. You should have said something.

CIARA awkwardly takes a sip of wine, because she's the one that knew every- thing from day 1, as she's got a separate WhatsApp chat with Nicola. She is the chosen one.

NICOLA

We weren't even sleeping in the same bed up until the last two months. It's like we were mates we didn't have sex in like–

CIARA

Maybe we should order you a taxi and get you home.

MARTINA

Home? I was going to grab her another glass of wine!? Let the woman speak! So how long did ya go without a ride? Carry on.

- Invite her to everything! Even the opening of an envelope. Sitting in her room feeling sorry for herself won't solve anything and could drive her back into the arms of her ex. Even if it's to help you with the food shop or accompany you to your gynaecology appointment. And also vice versa, I don't care if you're up for work at the crack of dawn, if she needs a night out, you go! Have no babysitter? Throw the child in the coat room. We're Irish, we were raised in pubs, on Coke and Tayto and it did us no harm.

- Big her up on her socials. Every time your friend posts a picture of herself, even if she looks half dead and dragged through a bus in it, like she fell from the ugly tree and hit every branch on her way down (*Jesus, Enya relax*), make sure you shower her with support and compliments. Make her feel like a prinny.

'Omg slayyyyy!'

'Wow!! 💧 💧 💧 💧 💧 💧 💧 💧 💧 💧'

'No sorry, I am deceased!'

'MILF'.

'I'm obsessed!!'

- Remain friends with your friend's ex on social media. Not because you were fond of him, but because he still follows you. Take advantage of this. Every time you're out with your friend and she looks *on fleek*, make sure you tag her and post her on your stories, bonus points if she looks like she's living her best life. Let the prick know what he's missing.

If you take anything away from this chapter, let it be this: your friend will notice your presence when it matters, and also your absence. Time is something money can't buy. She's your sister from another mister, and you are hers. Your friends will kiss a few frogs and ignore a few red flags along the way, but ultimately your nearest and dearest will always be there to pick up the pieces, so don't forget to return the favour. Imagine you're standing at the altar on your wedding day in years to come, with nobody by your side, even though you spent your childhood with these girls wearing pillowcases over your head and practising your aisle walks to Whitney Houston's *Greatest Love of All* in your mother's back bedroom. As the great Phoebe Buffay from *Friends* once said, 'Boyfriends and girlfriends are going to come and go, but *this* is for life.'

CHAPTER 3

Work Friends are in a League of their Own

They say friendships in the workplace can boost productivity, employee engagement and job satisfaction, in short, they make the whole nine to five ordeal pretty bearable. Over their working life, the average person will spend 70 per cent of their waking hours in work; in a lifetime, that's almost 90,000 hours!

Making friends at work is impossible to avoid since we spend so much of our time there. Just like when we were kids in school, we need someone to cling to for support and companionship. We need a buddy to pair up with. Your first day in a new job is very similar to the first day of school. You approach everyone with caution. Who will I gel with the most? Everyone you encounter during your induction you wonder about. Can this person handle my dark sense of humour? Does this person ever have the craic or are they just a robot? Is he really that attractive or is it just his aftershave?

Ironically, it's always the girl with the resting bitch face who looks like an absolute C U Next Tuesday, who ends up being the one you click with.

Whether it's a job in your twenties to get you by, or a career-defining opportunity in your thirties, the characteristics you desire in your work colleagues never really change. Remember your first job in the local supermarket? All you wanted was a group of people on your shift that made the day go by a bit quicker and who didn't take themselves too seriously. The same idea applies when you migrate to an office environment – meeting in the staff kitchen or the smoking area with your work bestie for a catch up to bitch about the lazy fuckers that keep everyone behind, or the narcissistic manager who has zero people skills make the day bearable. You've worked together so long that you develop nicknames for each staff member, in the event that they walk into the kitchen mid-bitch. It almost feels therapeutic that someone else is experiencing the same feelings you are and you're not imagining it. Trauma bonding, they call it. You could go home and vent to your boyfriend about Sensor Light (she only works when people walk by her desk), but he'll never truly understand the impact she has on your last nerve the way Becky from accounts, who can't stand the bitch either, can.

There's also that weird relationship you form with your manager or superior. For example, you had great craic with them at the company BBQ, you both had a little too much gin and ended up talking about everything from relationships to dieting advice. Then Monday comes around and they're blunt as a pencil, addressing your shit customer service skills. Has your manager just gaslit you? Saturday night she was all talk and very invested in your love life, to the point where you started to think asking for annual leave or calling in sick wouldn't seem as daunting anymore. You started to fantasize about holidaying together with your significant others and then the next minute she's passing you by in the corridor!

Whether it's in retail, in the office or out in the field here's a gentle reminder of colleagues you **do** want to befriend versus colleagues you **don't**!

Don't befriend:

The lazy fuck

There is nothing worse than working in retail in your early twenties, walking into an eight-hour shift on a Sunday morning, hungover from the night before, a pale face with a neck full of false tan, bloodshot eyes and your hair thrown into a hun bun, only to discover you and the *lazy fuck* are on shift together. Not only do you have to deal with the stupidity of the general public for the entire day, while trying not to gag every time someone brings a Red Bull up to the counter (Jagerbomb flashbacks from last night), but you also have to do the job of two people because Gary the snail takes three working days to complete a task. Your manager has left a list of thirty things to be completed before close and divided them up between the two of you.

ME

Okay, Gary, so we've to price up two hundred bumper bags of crisps. I'll do a hundred, and you do a hundred and we'll aim to do it in under an hour.

GARY

Yeah, no worries... I've a sore hand, so I'll try to be as quick as possible.

ME

Internally Oh fuck off, if there was work in the bed you'd sleep on the floor.

You've developed a system to price up products as quickly as possible, it's a habit at this stage, just like driving becomes easier through muscle memory. But because Gary the snail has to be difficult, he has invented a slower way of completing the task.

ME

Gary, if you sticker them up like this, it saves you so much more time.

GARY

Oh, I appreciate that. But I've always done it like this, and I've never had an issue.

ME

Nods and bites tongue, screaming internally to myself, never had an issue? The issue is it takes us three hours to do something that only takes one you absolute imbecile.

You couldn't be friends with someone like Gary, Gary brings out a rage in you you never knew was there. You don't know how patient you are until patience is your only option, apart from the option that gets you twenty-five to life in prison. If you were to hang out with Gary outside work, soon enough there'd be a Netflix documentary about how Gary the snail disappeared from his workplace never to be seen again.

The work rat

There's one in every workplace. I call them Trojan horses or Judas. They thrive on validation from figures of authority. In the early days you thought you could trust them, you thought they were being really friendly and helpful. Very chatty in the morning, specifically during breakfast time. (So chatty you never actually get to eat your oats and you stand there awkwardly holding your lunch box, subtly throwing hints that you'd like to eat your food in peace, until it's time to start work and they get shelved till lunch. They are always very interested in your weekend antics, holidays coming up, scandal on work nights out. You then learned the hard way that this person cannot be trusted. You could never prove it was that bitch that informed your manager that your nanny didn't really die (she died ten years ago, but when you start a new job, guess what, she's suddenly alive again!). You SAID needed the entire week of for the funeral processions (you were left with no other choice because your manager wouldn't give you the week off for an Ibiza trip with the girls. Sorry nanny, if you're looking down on me!) So, you decided to pull a Wagatha Christie and set up the work rat to prove your theory. You called in sick one Friday morning, made up an entire spiel about the local take-away being laced with salmonella, you were up all night, it was coming out of both ends. Then you found an old clip from a night out, downing shots of Tequila, on your snap chat, you set up a private story on Instagram, where only one person could view it. The Monday morning I was called into the office ...

Internal. Mid-Morning. An office block somewhere in Dublin City centre. (Can't be that hard to imagine.)

BOSS

Enya, I appreciate you coming into today's meeting. There are suspicions that you weren't sick on Friday, and you were OUT OUT on the Thursday. Meaning you were too hungover to come in to work. This is unacceptable

ME

Plays stupid What? Omg on a Thursday? Are you mad, not when *The Real Housewives of Beverly Hills* is streaming.

66

You'd never see me out on a Thursday. That's my pamper night, I shave every-thing, and change my sheets, Yankee can-dles, the lot.

BOSS

Well my source had video evidence.

Jackpot, the only person who had access to my private story was…. Splinter. I got off with a verbal warning (not because I faked a sickie, but because I laced Splinter's coffee with laxatives later that week.)

The HR wannabe

These people are such a pain in the hole. They take their job way too seriously. They never had the qualities or characteristics to progress to a managerial or supervisor role. So, they spend the rest of their days pretending to be one. They're the most vocal people in the work what's app group. They leave zero mistakes unnoticed.

The work WhatsApp group

Karen

Hi guys, good morning. I hate to be that person. If we could just clean up after ourselves when we finish

> eating our lunch in the kitchen, it would be greatly appreciated. Remember we all share this space to eat, so it's important to respect each other.

Milliseconds later

> **Karen**
>
> Hi guys, just a quick one. I know a lot of us are parents and have to do the school run in the mornings, but there's been a few latecomers this week for the morning shift, can I suggest trying to leave a bit earlier to beat the traffic or better yet, make your five-year-old walk to school by themselves in the torrential rain. When someone is late it can cause a knock-on effect for the rest of us who are already in work, under pressure with other tasks that need to be completed.

> **Me**
>
> *Mentally responding* Tasks? You sell scratch cards and smokes at the customer service desk, Karen. Get a grip.

The co-worker who will never swap shifts with you

These people obviously don't believe in Karma. And it's always at the most inconvenient time, when there's absolutely nobody left in the office or store who is available to swap with you. You're now left with your wan who doesn't believe in good deeds. It's your sister's big surprise party, or you need the morning off to recover from a family wedding, and you approach them a week beforehand, plenty of notice given, surely, they don't have plans on a Friday morning, you're praying for a miracle but also knowing your faith.

Internal. The staff kitchen. Mid-Morning.

ME

Hey, Michelle, I know this is a long shot, but my sister's wedding is next Thursday, I completely forgot to book the following day off, and there's nobody available other than you who could work it. Is there any chance you could take my shift and I'll return the favour when you need it? You know yourself, there's nothing worse than having an eight-hour shift hanging over you when you're trying to enjoy a night out.

MICHELLE

Aw, no way! You should have come to me

about an hour ago, I told my mother-in-law I'd help her alphabetise her Disney DVD collection.

ME

Who still collects DVDs, didn't they die with Xtravision? Oh, okay, it's just I remember when your fella dumped you via text while we were on shift together last month and I stayed on for an extra eight hours and covered for you when I could have gone home. But no worries.

MICHELLE

It's a really big Disney collection...

ME

No worries, I'll just remember to not do anything nice for anyone ever again, EVER.

Don't befriend people like Michelle, they are of no benefit to you in the workplace and think of nobody but themselves and have no empathy for the suffering of other people. People like

Michelle were always picked last in PE and now want to take it out on their work colleagues. It's an abuse of power. Don't be like Michelle.

The fella who flirts with every girl he's on shift with, even though he's in a relationship with somebody outside the workplace

This man will prey on vulnerable women who love a red flag and have a history of dating players. Similar to a male peacock showing off their flamboyant feathers to attract a mate, this lad will bathe in Dior Sauvage. The smell is so overpowering, the women he targets won't have time to contemplate if engaging with this lad is worth the heartache. He'll play every girl in the workplace like a fiddle, until he gets the ride after a work night out, and then move onto his next target. Don't befriend someone like this, they only have one thing on their mind and it's because they're allergic to commitment. However, if you'd like some advice on relationships, he would be the best person to go to, just do the opposite of everything he advises you to do.

Do befriend:

The workplace comedian

Usually they're called Anto. These people are the saving grace in a toxic workplace. If it wasn't for them, the office or shop floor

71

would be a dark place. They show up every day in such a positive mood with a pep in their step. They have the balls to take the piss out of the Garys, the Splinters, and the Michelles of the workplace and tell them to their faces what we all think of them.

Internal. Shop floor. Anto spots Gary stocking the shelves, in a painfully slow fashion beside a co-worker who is stocking the shelves in record time.

ANTO

Jesus Gary, you're going slower than me nanny, and she's dead fourteen years.

GARY

Just trying to kill more time so I don't have to go back on the tills.

ANTO

What's the expiry date on them tins of peas?

GARY

Eh, next June.

ANTO

You be lucky to be done by July at your going rate.

Internal. A busy staff kitchen during lunch.

SPLINTER

Need tomorrow off! Got last-minute tickets for the match, my young fella has been dying to see these play.

ANTO

Michelle, will cover for you, won't you Michelle? Oh, that's right you can't, you're watching your grass grow.

KAREN

Ha, ha!!

ANTO

Karen, can you loan me your ladder?

KAREN

What ladder?

ANTO

The one you use to climb up HR's arse?

Befriending someone like Anto in the workplace has been proven to improve your mood and productivity. He's great at making stressful situations seem less stressful. He makes a great salesman because everyone is attracted to a sense of humour and a bit of confidence. That's why he's more likely to get a co-worker's phone number compared to the Dior Sauvage influencer. Everyone wants to sit at his table at conferences and staff nights out. Befriending him also means he's less likely to take the piss out of you.

The Lifer

In the working world there is no such thing as too old or too young when it comes to befriending people. You could be twenty-five and your work bestie could be a fifty-seven-year-old reception-ist called Sharon who's been in the company twenty-five years. They become your life, financial and relationship consultant all wrapped up in one.

Internal. Reception area. Morning.

ME

Morning, Sharon! Did you enjoy your

cruise with the hubby? Back to pissy Irish weather!

SHARON

It was brilliant, I got you the cigarettes in the duty free for your ma. Are you coming to bingo later? I'll fill you in.

ME

I wouldn't miss it for the world. I found those boots; remember the ones I said I was going to root out for you?

External. Smoking area. Afternoon

ME

So, yeah, I don't know what to do. We've been arguing a lot lately.

SHARON

Let me tell you something, love, I've been around men longer than you've been breathing air, and you're going to come across a lot of time-wasters and eejits.

Don't rush it, what's meant to be will be. The number of times I broke up and got back together with my Tony when I was your age until he finally had the balls to put a ring on it. Mind you I was pregnant at the time, and that's what you had to do, but the sentiment was still nice.

The person you get along with most – aka your work bestie

In every large group of people, it's human nature to gravitate toward someone who has a lot in common with you, similar age, sense of humour and morals. Somebody who just *gets* you. What starts off as a few polite conversations in the staff room, turns into adding each other on social media, going out for your first lunch together, sharing the same hatred for another co-worker, in fact sometimes your initial bond is rooted in your hatred for another colleague! When you start to hang out with them outside of work, you have now acquired a work bestie. There are now no professional boundaries between you two – that ship sailed on day two of getting to know each other.

Qualities of a work bestie

- They can be trusted - The nosy bitch brigade at work would love to know about your pregnancy scare in the toilets this afternoon (which is why you had to leave a meeting earlier to throw up) or the verbal warning you received from HR for sending dark-humour memes into the work chat. Only your bestie gets to know this information, while everyone else is none the wiser.

- Reliability - They have absolutely no issue staying back to help you out with extra workload or swapping a shift with you due to an impending hangover, because that's what work besties do; you scratch my back, I scratch yours.

- They always keep you in the loop - If you're away on annual leave or just have a day off, you can guarantee you'll receive a breakdown of how the day went in your absence. 'Guess who called in sick for the fifth day in a row?', 'Just so you know, there's murder over someone robbing them gluten-free yogurts from the fridge, be prepared to be interrogated when you come in tomorrow.'

- They'll always have your back - They'll never let someone in the office or on the shop floor speak out of turn about you while you're not around and will defend you until death. That's when you know they're a real one.

- They're good craic - There's nothing worse than being surrounded by people who take their career seriously 24/7. Work besties lighten the mood, share inside jokes, and create camaraderie that makes work life a more pleasant place to be.

Now that we've established the people we should and shouldn't befriend in the workplace, let's talk about when all of these headcases are in the same room together under the influence of alcohol. That's right, you guessed it, the work Christmas party. It's not for the faint-hearted. It reminds me of going into secondary school and learning how much fun the Debs in sixth year would be; then it was all I could think about for those next six years. Just make it through your Junior Cert and you're halfway to your debs! The work Christmas party is similar: even though each day in this hellhole is soul destroying, it's now September which means I've only three more months to go until I get my One 4 All gift voucher and an open bar.

The build-up to the staff Christmas party begins around October. A WhatsApp group is established as per usual and suggestions are thrown out. Some lucky bitch from HR gets the gift of putting it together. There'll always be one or two who want to play it safe ('Let's go to this restaurant, my sister's husband owns it, and the lobster is immaculate!') vs the interns who would rather go somewhere that's more their scene ('Can we not book an area in that new bar they do two-for-one on the Sambuca shots and the finger food is lovely.') You'll eventually meet somewhere in the middle: a decent place for food and a reserved area in a popular bar.

If there's a downside to a Christmas party, it's the Kris Kindle presentation at work the day of the party. You will without a doubt end up buying a gift for someone you know absolutely nothing about. That man who works from home four days a week and sits in the corner of the office with his headphones on. Lynx sets are always a safe bet. You only wish you could have got Sharon; a few scratch cards and twenty Blue would have lit her face up like a Christmas tree.

Things to expect at a work Christmas party:

- Witnessing the mute in the office make a holy show of themselves on Karaoke. Have you ever looked at somebody and thought, *There's no way they're that perfect. Something's got to give.* You've never heard them speak, they're always on time for work, always meet deadlines, never call in sick, etc. Just give them the gift of an endless bottle of wine and you'll soon realize that they can't handle their drink. They let loose one day of the year, butcher a Whitney song and end up in a taxi before midnight. They'll be working from home for the foreseeable until it's a distant memory for anyone who was present that night.

- The one who's driving. There will always be someone who either never drinks or chooses not to drink at the work Christmas party (even though it's free!) This person has either enjoys watching other people destroy their reputation with the boss, or else just despises everyone they work with and cannot stand to be in their presence unless being paid to do so. If you suffer from the beer fear, maybe avoid the only sober person at the party, they'll remember everything when Monday morning comes around. They'll usually do an Irish goodbye before midnight and slip out undetected.

- You'll befriend someone from a different department that you never have the intention of speaking to ever again. Everyone is a lot more social after a few drinks, especially the smoking area. You'll get chatting to someone and come to realize that you've now got a face to put to all those emails about conduct in the workplace. 'Oh, *you're* Jenny!! It's nice to finally meet you!' You'll initially bond over how anti-social you both are, but feel obliged to attend these events, her husband will then come over to join the conversation, and pretend he doesn't recognise you, but you immediately recognise him, because he tried it on you at the company BBQ.

- Doing shots with the CEO. The only time you see this man or woman is when they are in a boardroom projecting the company's financial year ahead. Seeing them buy a round of shots for the accounts team is like seeing a teacher outside of school. It's strange. But also it gives you a reality check that they're human too.

• Catch two people in the act. Have you ever heard a sober person say that nothing good happens after midnight? Well at work events, that's when all the scandals come to fruition. They say drinking impairs your decision making, but also your ability to stay faithful to your wife or husband. The two people who are constantly flirting under your nose on the shop floor or in the office, have now confirmed your speculation, they are in fact riding. In the coat closet to be exact. Aul Splinter and Dior Savage.

Although remote working is becoming the norm since the pandemic began in 2020, I'm all for workplace friendships! Humans are social creatures, and although you won't be besties with everyone in your workplace, having someone who understands the stress your job entail is key to keeping your sanity. Working from home and not having a face-to-face connection must be shite after a while! It reminds me of when I was in school. I'd love getting the day off when I was sick, but by day two, it became boring real fast, sitting at home watching *Judge Judy*, alone, was zero craic. I'd actually rather be back in class learning all about the slope of a line in the company of the class clowns.

Have you ever heard that there's three versions of you: the version only you see behind closed doors, the version your friends and family see, and the version strangers know when you're out in public? Well, I'd like to add a fourth: the version only your co-workers see. My best mate will never have to give me a pep talk before I go into a board room full of directors, to give them a career-defining presentation, after a night of work drinks, that was only supposed to be 'just the one'. My best mate would never understand the type of people I have to deal with!

ENYA

How am I going to do this presentation,
and not get sick! I can't do this, I can't!!

JANET

You'll be grand! Karen and Splinter are
working from home today, so only I can
get the whiff of pure ethanol from you.
Here take a spray of this!

Drowns me in a Zara Dupe perfume

Massive isn't it? Saved €80 and it fits
in me bag! Now, get loads of caffeine

into you, a pastry and you'll fly it. Have you been practising your posh accent? They really bought into it the last time! Talk about going to the theatre and your tennis lessons, that will sweeten them up, that creepy aul fella was loving it. If all else fails and you run out of steam up there, show a bit of cleavage and you'll be grand. I'll nip to Spar and leave you a Lucozade a few hash browns on your desk for afterwards. We go for a vape down at the shelter.

Work friends, they're in a league of their own!

CHAPTER 4

Navigating the Female WhatsApp Group

We have all our friends at our fingertips these days! More than twenty years after PC chat rooms I'm going to go full Nanny here and say, 'I remember the original social group. MSN, we called it, and you'd have to sit at a desktop computer. It was this big box with a screen, and it had a keyboard. I must try to find a photo of it on my iPhone 57. I think they dug one up there recently and put it in the *National Museum of Throwbacks*. Back then you couldn't go about your day and read messages on the go, like you can now. You'd have to have a conversation in one position, sitting stooped over a desk. If you wanted to meet your friends in the park, you'd have to warn them you're about to leave the house, because there'd be no way of contacting them once you left your house, you'd just have to hope they wouldn't stand you up.'

But as technology advanced, so did social media, from Myspace to MSN, to Bebo, to Facebook. Smartphones are now your house phone and your PC all in one; you can do everything on them! You can use the internet on the go, listen to music, watch videos, listen to podcasts, facetime your mates in the middle of a sky dive, even on some planes! We Now have Instagram, Snapchat, and finally (so far!) WhatsApp.

You can see when someone was last active, you can see if someone saw your message and decided to open or not open. Blue tick, grey tick, she's a tick… or even worse, blocked!

'Why does the fella I've been casually seeing, suddenly have no profile picture on WhatsApp?'

There is no hiding! Thinking of throwing a surprise party for your mate? Great, let me start a WhatsApp group with two hundred people from far and wide and absolutely wallop you with a hundred notifications an hour about how to set up the perfect diversion so Mary doesn't know she's on the way to her own surprise party. Sometimes I wish I could go back to the 'call me' days or even receive a party invitation by post. There is no hiding, your digital footprint is everywhere!

It's the norm to be part of some type of *group*, from Work, Surprise parties, Holiday planning, Hen/Stag Parties etc.

But what is it like being part of the girls' WhatsApp group?

Ah, the female WhatsApp group — a fascinating social phenomenon that has emerged in the digital age. Join me, Enya Attenborough, as we explore this intricate world and observe its behaviours.

Having a nose into the habitat

In the vast digital ecosystem, WhatsApp groups thrive as interconnected communities of women with shared interests, purposes, or affiliations. Much like a flock of those bleedin' magpies or a colony of feral cats, members of a female WhatsApp group come together, forging bonds and exchanging information within the confines of a virtual space. (*Look at me with all my posh words, you'd never think I got a D3 in Higher Level English in the Leaving Cert.*)

Let us first observe the creation of a WhatsApp group. A group emerges when an individual assumes the role of a 'group administrator' and this female invites others to join. This action initiates the formation of a microcosm (had to use the thesaurus for that one) a virtual habitat where participants interact and communicate.

Within these groups, a diverse range of species can be found. There are the 'Active Contributors,' who enthusiastically share their thoughts, opinions (some a bit too opinionated), and multimedia content such as memes. These individuals are the lifeblood of the group, driving conversations and fostering a sense of community.

For example, there has been an ongoing discussion in the group throughout the weeks based on the neighbour who is a suspected drug dealer.

Martina

There's no way he's able to drive a BMW 5 series on a builder's wages, girls!

Nicola

He's off on holidays again girls, Dubai!

> **Mary**
>
> Jaysus, I might get into the labouring meself!

> **Martina**
>
> His mot defo got a BBL in Turkey, never saw her in a gym in my life. Only way you'd get an arse like that is by squatting 80kg on your back five days a week.

Video evidence has now surfaced from an unknown source, who filmed the whole ordeal at 6am as said neighbour was getting a thorough raid from the Criminal Assets' Bureau. The active contributor is quite like TMZ; they have the video evidence before anyone else in the community.

However, we must also acknowledge the presence of the 'Silent Observers' or 'The Lurkers.' These members, similar to the hidden creatures of the forest, prefer to remain on the periphery, silently absorbing the group's discussions without actively participating. They may occasionally emerge from the shadows to react or respond, but their primary role is that of passive observers. These species are similar to those who set up an Instagram, Facebook, Snapchat or a TikTok profile, but don't post anything, just watch everything! The ghosts of social media, one might call them.

Like any ecosystem, WhatsApp groups have their own set of dynamics and hierarchies. At the top of the food chain, we find the group administrators. The role they play in the friend group can range from: everything is left for them to organize such as parties, holidays, nights out, because they believe other members of the group are not competent to fulfil such tasks. They hold the power to regulate access, manage memberships, and enforce rules. Administrators are akin to the alpha animals, guiding the group's direction and maintaining order.

Now, let us explore the communication patterns within these groups. Participants engage in a variety of behaviours, such as:

Posting humorous memes:

Mary

There's you on a Sunday morning Martina heading for your breakfast roll.

Engaging in lively debates:

Mary

Girls, any good boxset recommendations?

Sinead

Yeah, *The Last Heartbreak* on Netflix is very good, I watched it all in a day!

Nicola

Ah, Sinead that was bleeding shite, I turned it off after 1 episode.

Sinead

It takes a while for you to understand it, bit mad at first but you start to enjoy it a bit more as time goes on.

Nicola

How your fella ended up with you, is it?

The exchange of messages can be rapid and continuous, resembling a cacophony of voices in a tropical rainforest.

1am

Sinead

Girls, just home from the first date...

Sinead is recording....

Nicola

'What!?'

Shauna

Ah come on Shino, spit it out, sitting here 5 minutes, dying to hear all about it.

Mary

Was he a catfish?

Nicola

Did he pay!?

Mary

It's late enough, must have gone well if it was 6 hours long.

Nicola

Either that, or she's more patient than we thought.

Shauna

What aftershave was he wearing.

Mary

Is she still bleedin' recording?

The consultancy role of the What's App group

The female WhatsApp group also acts as a consultancy firm when it comes to romantic relationships, specifically during relationship conflict. For example, one of your friends may be having issues with their significant other and they are seeking support in how to deal with this situation. As a woman myself, I understand our tendency to press the *psychopath activate* button, as our first instinct, but we usually liaise with our friends and establish alternative routes before we still decide to press the *Psychopath Activate* button. I think it's healthy to have a balance of friends who love carnage and friends who think rationally in situations like this; it helps you see the issue from both sides. At the end of the day, our besties are our real soulmates!

A scenario as such would go like this:

Nicola

Girls, am I overreacting here or what? I asked him if I looked better in the *red or black* dress and he said *I think the black one suits you more,* what the f**k!? What's wrong with the red one? Do I not look attractive in the red one or something?

Mary

Always say, *both!*

Nicola

Don't even feel like going out now, threatening to get in my pjs, but he keeps telling me I'm overreacting,

telling me I *shouldn't have asked if I didn't want an*
answer.

Martina

I hate when they challenge you with logic! Prick...

Sarah

Maybe he was showing genuine interest and wanted
to form an opinion before he answered. Imagine you
went out and didn't feel comfortable in the red dress,
you'd be glad he gave his opinion.

Martina

Ah, go away you, with your healthy relationship.

Nicola

What will I do?

Martina

Go out but just give him the silent treatment until he
grovels for forgiveness, let him work for it, the prick.

Sarah

Don't let it ruin your date night, you've been looking forward to it all week.

Nicola

You're right, Sarah, but I'm still going to make him feel like shit.

When you have a fight with your boyfriend, you can always rely on that one friend who knows basic grammar to articulate a strongly worded WhatsApp essay to him (he thinks it's from you, obviously!) They have the ability to present your argument in a logical and compelling manner, they'll use facts, evidence and persuasive language to convince your boyfriend about the validity of your claims. They'll maintain a mature tone throughout, avoiding personal attacks or offensive language, while your other friends are a liability with this one!

Martina

Just tell him, you can shove this relationship up your hole, ya fool! Send that to him!

Skilled friend

No, no, noooo, you want to come across as the calm

and collected one, you're not supposed to be bothered by all this, the less bothered you come across the
less likely he is to retaliate and misunderstand your
point of view. Men think with their balls not their brain.
Don't reveal everything you know in your opening
statement, save some bullets for the cross examina-
tion! So, this is what you say...

They conduct thorough research on the topic before forming
your essay. They'll use a calm tone throughout and choose their
words wisely, 'I respect your stance on the situation, however...'
or 'I wanted to bring some concerns to your attention and I'm
hoping we can work through these together.'

It then turns into a game of tennis with screenshots from the
private chat between you and your boyfriend who is oblivious
that the board of directors are discussing your responses thor-
oughly. Your skilled friend is working overtime here! She should
have been a barrister, but instead she's got to carry on the family
business name and ended up as a funeral director. Someone's
poor nanny is being laid out to rest in room 2b and your barrister
friend is behind a desk, in another world, preparing to go to trial
against your boyfriend.

The skilled friend

OK, this is what I've come up with. Send him this and make him feel like shit! 'Heya, I need to talk to you about something that's been bothering me, I want to start by saying I'm not angry, but I am disappointed. When you made comments about my weight, it really hurt. I don't think you understand how sensitive women can be about their bodies and the impact that words like that can have.

It's not just about what you said, but how it made me feel, it's important to be mindful of the things we say to each other, especially when it comes to sensitive topics. I know you probably didn't mean any harm, but it's still something that shouldn't be brushed off.

I hope you can understand where I'm coming from and we can have a conversation about this. Communication is key in any relationship and I want us to be able to talk openly and honestly with each other.'

Martina

Yeah, it's just missing a few C U Next Tuesdays

Nicola

Oh I love it! I'm sending him that now!

Moments later, Nicola assumes she's replied to the group:

Nicola

This is what the dope is after saying! 'Holy Jaysus, women are mad, When did I even say anything about your weight? Making stuff up again, as usual. I said sorry and I'm not dragging this out any further. Ridiculous.' Girls I am sooo tempted to go to town on him about his morning breath, his cow of a mother and his inbred Jack Russel!

Him

You know you sent that to me?

*Cue **CODE BLACK!!** in the group*

We've all been there. Throw your phone in the canal, get a taxi to the airport and leave the country. Say your goodbyes, dye your hair, form a new identity, start a new life. Never return.

Emojis

Within this digital habitat, certain rituals and social norms have evolved. These include the use of emojis to convey emotions. An insult can be construed as malicious or light-hearted without the use of an emoji. For example, the Lurker friend decides to make their monthly guest appearance:

Aoife

They have those black boots back in Penney's, girls, in case you were still looking for them.

Sarah

Aoife, nice of you to join us today, good to know you're still alive, was convinced you removed yourself

---

The creation of inside jokes that foster group cohesion:

Mary

Girls, saw Skid Mark in the cinema tonight, Sinead you really did get a lucky escape. In saying that, he raised his standards, judging by his new mot.

Shauna

Ah leave Skid Mark alone, he gave us great material in this group, I still listen back to the audio messages that night she found his boxers.

Sinead

Mary, F off you!

And the occasional eruption of conflicts, reminiscent of territorial disputes in the animal kingdom:

Sinead

Can we not go somewhere else for food other than Murphy's kitchen, I'm sick of eating them BLTs.

Mary

It's cheap and nearby, unless you want to pay an arm and a leg somewhere else.

Sinead

Mary, you only want to go because you think the fella behind the till is mad about ya: we found him on social media and my mate in the revenue got his PPS number – he has a wife and kids!

Aoife

Nobody likes breaking data-protection rules either.

Sinead

Oh, hi, Aoife, nice of you to check in!

Mary

Well I'm going to Murphy's; you can go somewhere else if it's such an issue.

Aoife

Ah here, you can all come over to mine for lunch. Now shut up the pair of you.

Sinead

Love the sound of screaming kids, while I'm trying to inhale my soup.

Sinead is recording …

Mary

Here we go.

The challenges and dangers of the WhatsApp jungle.

Tensions may arise due to differences in opinion, misunderstandings, efforts to organize a night out (a separate chapter in itself!) or breaches of group etiquette.

For example, a member of the group has experienced something traumatic: they had ordered their holiday clothes online and they only arrived after said person departed for their holiday. *The lurker* chimes in blissfully unaware of what horrible ordeal has just taken place.

Mary

Girls, what am I going to do? €200 I spent on those outfits, brought the ring light and all with me for the new profiler, and can't even wear any of them. They're sitting at home in my kitchen and I'm sitting over here in Tenerife.

Sinead

Look, get a drink into you, you're on holiday, what's done is done. Just try enjoying yourself.

Nicola

You might have to wear the same outfit twice, but so what, just don't take any pictures the second time.

Sinead

Right, let's not jump to conclusions, Nicola ffs.

Shauna

I can't imagine what you're going through, thinking of you at this awful time.

Nicola

Surely there's a shopping centre nearby? My aunty knows the owner of the Aul Triangle pub, she might have a dress or two you can borrow.

Aoife

Girls, what oven temperature would you cook a turkey at?

Nicola

Time and place, Aoife!

> **Aoife**
>
> What did I miss? Oh Mary, are you away? Hope you enjoy yourself, take loads of pics!

Yet despite occasional conflicts, these groups have proven to be resilient, adapting to the ever-changing digital landscape. Such as voice messages. However, here's a *very* big difference between sending a quick twenty-second voice message and the actual podcasts some people send! Do they love the sound of their own voices? The worst kind is when your friend sounds like they're in the middle of a building site:

MARY

'What time can I go for food?' Emmm, sorry, just in the middle of cleaning here, ever get when you just start something and can't stop! Oh, hold on the baby is trying to eat something off the floor, That's bold Shania! That's dirty, stop that! Will I turn on *Coco Melon*? Good girl, now sit there while Mammy talks to her friend.

At one point in time, once something was posted online or

into a group it was there forever! However, the introduction of several new WhatsApp features has without a doubt changed the game in how people interact!

Deleting messages before the other person has seen them.

I think this is an absolute game changer, especially if you don't have the help of a highly skilled friend to fight your battles when it comes to boyfriend drama, or you accidentally drunk-text your work colleague one Saturday night. Now all WhatsApp has to do is not notify someone that you deleted a message, it looks so sketchy!

In conclusion, WhatsApp groups are intricate ecosystems where individuals with similar interests come together to interact, share information, and build communities. They represent a unique blend of human social dynamics and the digital age. I, Enya Attenborough, am constantly fascinated by the interconnected-ness of our world, whether it be in the natural realm or the digital realm of WhatsApp groups.

CHAPTER 5

When the Girls' Holiday Makes it out of the Group Chat

What to expect when the girls' holiday finally makes it out of the group chat? Let's establish how the idea of a holiday usually surfaces.

Scenario One:

You're having a catch-up over a bottle of wine at one of the girls' houses. The summer evenings are always the best for wine o'clock.

One of your mates, usually the one with the most disposable income, will have a big back garden with comfortable patio furniture and one of them fire pits you see on the likes of *Love Island* ('all for bleedin' show!' as my mother would say.) The kids are with their dad or their grandparents, so you can be loud and giddy just like your old teenage selves. Listening to old-school bangers, you'll laugh and reminisce about old times, old teachers, old boyfriends, friends who have come and gone from your lives. Then somebody brings up the first girls' holiday you all went on in your early twenties... No matter how many times you talk about it, it will never get old.

ENYA

OMG remember the flight going over? We were lucky not to be thrown off.

SARAH

No, remember that barman in Molly Malones who was mad about me? I'm still friends with him on Facebook; he has a wife and kids now!

SINEAD

Remember my room getting robbed and

we had to sit in the police station for hours with a translator? Holiday insurance my hole, I still never got a penny back ten years later!

ENYA

Remember we brought those two lads from Cork back to the room and one of them blocked the toilet!?

And then someone drops the bomb and ignites the fire...

SINEAD

Ah, girls, we have to go back to Tenerife again...

MARY

Girls, you know me I'm up for anything. Give me enough notice I can book it off my work calender.

SARAH

I've no holidays planned for next summer

so if we book it asap, I've no excuses.

SINEAD

I finally paid off my credit union loan so I'm due another one soon!

ENYA

I'm well up for that, what time of year are we thinking? Will I price flights now? What about June, might get a bit cheaper as kids are still in school and it's not peak season?

SARAH

I'll have to check my work calendar, but if it's free I can do June.

For the remainder of the evening, the holiday goo is in full swing, you all agree on the ideal week, ideal flights and ideal hotel.

ENYA

We will put a deposit down tomorrow, you

all just Revolut me your split and I'll book
it on my card. Delighted now, something
to look forward to. Life's too short girls,
book it while we can.

It's time to go home, you share a taxi with one of your friends
and you're already looking up SHEIN for the holiday bits, talking
shite and still heavily sedated with Pinot Grigio.

SINEAD

Ah, I'm living for this now; a girls' holiday is long overdue. I'll have to go back
to the gym and get my bikini body back.

SARAH

I'll be cornering me ma tomorrow about
minding the kids that week. Now, Ma
I'm giving you nearly a year's notice! No
excuses, I haven't had a holiday with my
mates in years.

SINEAD

Anywhere along here is grand, Mr Taxi
Driver. Right, good night and God bless.

I'll Facetime you tomorrow and we'll book this once and for all.

Then tomorrow rolls around. You've sobered up after a solid eight-hour sleep (because you're the only one in the group who's baby free.) You pick up your phone just like you would the morning paper and see what's new on social media. A WhatsApp message from one of the girls draws your attention.

> **Sarah**
>
> Flights €350 return, hotel €300 each. What are we thinking?

Your first thought is, *Oh no, what have I agreed to? I've got about ten weddings coming up, I'm struggling to afford finance on this new car as it is and I'm saving for a house. Oh no, no, noooo. Damn you, white wine! What did you agree to on my behalf!?*

> **Sinead**
>
> I think that's the best deal we're going to get. Enya, you're very quiet this morning. What do you think?

Enya

Oh, girls what was I even saying last night? I've loads coming up, after thinking about it I don't think I'll pull it off with everything else coming up this year, so book this one without me.

Sinead

Ah, come on you dry shite, you were all for it last night!! Only dry shites back out.

Enya

I genuinely can't afford it right now.

Mary

Sorry, girls, I'm in work right now, I'll catch up on these later.

Sarah

I'll loan you the deposit and you can pay me back after the holiday.

Ok, I'm fucked now I've no excuse!

> **Enya**
>
> Ugh, fine... but can we price May, maybe we can get it cheaper?

Congratulations, the holiday has made it through the first stage. Booking it.

It's about three months before the holiday, it's all you talk about on WhatsApp or when you get together once in a blue moon. There are holiday memes in abundance in the group chat... But then, one morning you get that dreaded text:

> **Mary**
>
> Hey girls, you'll never guess what? I'm having another baby! I'm due next March, which means I won't be able to go on the holiday. I obviously didn't plan this, and I'm devastated I can't go, but by all means you all still go, you aren't the ones that are pregnant, lol!

Unfortunately, everyone knows it won't be the same holiday with three amigos instead of all four. This results in the holiday falling apart and everyone losing their deposit – €250 we will never see again, because someone couldn't keep their legs closed. Also to blame is that certain someone who had to open their big mouth one August evening out a back garden after a few bevvies. I hope you're happy, Sinead.

Scenario Two

Then of course you have the girls' holiday that's planned in a sober state of mind. It's been a long time coming, five or six years since your last get-together abroad. And you all kept saying, *we'll have to book it, we'll have to get around to it*. And that day finally arrives when someone just takes the bull by the horns and shows some initiative.

> **Enya**
> Girls, who is up for a holiday next summer? You all have six months' notice so no excuses with the kids, come on, you deserve a break!

Everyone collectively agrees a holiday is indeed needed. Getting people to agree to a holiday is the easy part. Deciding where, what, how and when among friends with totally different lifestyle and financial situations is the hard part. I (certainly not by choice) end up being the organizer appointed by the WhatsApp group.

Sinead

Enya, will you look up the flights there, I'm just at work.

Sarah

Yeah, Enya, keep us in the loop, try to use Skyscanner if you can and we get a cheap and cheerful option.

And that's how simple it is to become the group-appointed holiday booker! Looking up flights turns into looking up hotels, looking up locations, taking everyone's passport details, using your card to book for everyone, chasing people for money and so on. The booker is also the friend who will show up to the restaurant early to save the reservation, while everyone else arrives late. We are the backbone of the friend group. Organizing a holiday is very similar to organizing a night out with your friends.

I just want a week away in the sun, I never asked for any of this responsibility. Try to recall holidays in your early twenties. Nobody gave a shit where or when you went, it just mattered who you went with. You'd gladly stay in some dodgy shithole that had one star on Tripadvisor, every review starting with 'Avoid!!' or else 'Place stinks of weed!' But you didn't give a shit because you were all on a budget with your part-time jobs, and you'd end up drinking yourselves into oblivion most of the time you were there because that was the cool thing to do at that age, so you would be ignorant to the fact that several people were murdered in your hotel over the years, and the cleaners were professionals when it came to room robberies and inside jobs. But when you're on a good wage and can afford to stay somewhere more upscale, or afford the extra luxuries of a nice pool, room view, restaurants, you become *way* pickier.

The organizer friend: 'Ok, ladies I think I found a good deal! Lanzarote, hotel on the beach, strip is lively, June 7th - 14th €650, online special.'

Tight Friend: '€650 is a bit steep.'

Blames her fella friend: 'He's away on a stag that weekend, I won't be able to get the kids minded.'

The thirty-year-old who still parties like she's eighteen friend: 'Is Lanzarote not full of old people?'

The shitter friend: 'Hate to be that person, I went there last year, and my room got robbed, could we try somewhere else?'

The unemployed friend: Can we not book it on a site where you can pay in instalments?

The tight friend: 'Why don't we just go on a weekend away to Newcastle or London or something. Cheap and cheerful.'

On the verge of breakdown if she doesn't take a week off from the job she hates, friend: 'Are you for real? Newcastle? I've been breaking my bollox at work all year. I've had a pain in me hole changing dirty nappies day in, day out, in that crèche. I need a strawberry daiquiri by a pool in 30-degree heat and a bikini that's far too tight on me, not sitting in a manky pub somewhere in the UK, in miserable weather, for nearly double the money, when I could do that in Ireland any weekend of the year, If I've to swim to the Canaries by myself, I will!'

The organizer friend: 'So the flight going over is at 5pm...'

The tight friend: 'Ah, sure the day will be gone by the time we get there, so we're basically only getting six days there.'

The organizer friend: 'There's another flight at 7am.'

The tight friend: 'Ah, sure then you're getting up in the middle of the night, only two hours sleep, you'll be wrecked the whole first day.'

The thirty-year-old who still parties like she's eighteen friend: 'Are you thirty or sixty-five?'

After going back and forth with the group for what will feel like eternity, you'll finally agree on a date and location. A lot of sacrifices and rejigging had to be made, but you got there in the end, and nobody left the group chat out of spite or anger. The friendship and group are still intact.

Departures

When the week of your girls' holiday finally rolls around, everybody is bursting with excitement. It's finally here! Nails done, hair dyed, extensions in, tan on fleek and last few bits bought. The usual group liaison about what you're wearing to the airport starts happening.

Enya
I'm wearing a playsuit.

Sinead
Oh, will that not be a bastard to get out of when using the toilet on the plane?

Sarah

I'm wearing denim shorts and a crop top.

Sinead

Would the denim shorts not be uncomfortable to wear on a plane?

Enya

Ah, Sinead, you're probably going in the nip at this rate.

Ciara

Did anyone book in to get their makeup done before the airport?

(FYI Ciara jumped in on the holiday at the last minute because she broke up with her fella, and wants a hot girl summer, and a Spanish rebound.)

Enya

Ah here, makeup and a fashion show? I don't give a shite what I wear, just get me to the Garden Terrace

> Bar for a drink and I'll be happy. I'm pissed just thinking about it, roll on!

> **Sarah**
>
> Two more days in work and I get to turn on that *out of office* email!!

The day of the holiday arrives, it's 7am and the pre-booked taxi from six months ago does a pit stop at every house. It's like an episode of *Catfish*, watching your friends walk out the front door facetuned to bits with the flawless filter foundation, because you know they'll look like the back of a bus going back into through their front door in seven days time.

One of your poor friends is always stuck in the front of the seven-seater with the taxi driver, while the craic is ninety in the back. The cheap bottle of pure piss is getting passed around, for everyone to take a swig out of, and then the million-dollar question gets put on the table.

SINEAD

How much sleep did you all get?

CIARA

Oh, by the time I got everything ready it was two in the morning!

ENYA

Sleep? You all went to sleep? You'll sleep when you're dead! I was watching that show *Magaluf Weekender* to get me in the mood.

SARAH

I was in bed at eleven last night, I took a Nytol, and I was out for the count.

SINEAD

And we all checked in, yeah? Are we all sitting together?

ENYA

I just selected a random seat; sure, the flight is only two and a half hours.

SINEAD

Won't pay €6.00 to sit beside her friends

on the plane, but will happily spend about
€100 on drink and perfume in the duty
free.

SARAH

Ah, you two better not be like this for the
whole week, I'm not getting stuck in the
middle of it like last time.

Every single girl was warned in the group chat before the taxi
arrived this morning to bring cash. And yet someone still managed to not have cash on them.

ENYA

Girls, will someone cover me, and I'll get
them a drink on the plane?

SINEAD

Wonder where I've heard that before...

When a group of girls pack for a holiday, they will *always* over
pack. Especially underwear for some reason? We always envision
the worst-case scenario, but also the most unrealistic. *Okay, I'm
going away for seven days, but what happens if I piss myself every day*

for seven consecutive days? Or what happens if I randomly get a very heavy period even though my cycle doesn't start until two weeks after I'm home? Better pack twenty-one pairs of knickers. Okay, but what happens if my suitcase goes missing? Better pack twenty-one pairs in my carry-on case too.

Underwear is acceptable to overpack. However, there will always be a friend who finds their bag is 10kg over the limit. The emotionally sterile attendant delivers the bad news.

>   DESK GIRL
> You're over by 10kg, and it's a tenner
> per kg. Card or cash?

>   ENYA
> Ah, wtf, Sinead did you not weigh it at
> home?

>   SINEAD
> I didn't have a scale!

>   SARAH
> How is it 10kg over? Wtf did you pack?

> *Sinead opens her bag and fifty pairs of*

shoes, and ten bun bags spill out onto the
floor, along with a jumbo bottle of Listerine.

ENYA

How many pairs of sandals did you bring?
Are you flogging them at the beach over
there?

SARAH

What's with the jumbo bottle of mouth-
wash?

ENYA

She's opening a dental practice on the
strip.

SINEAD

You can all shove a pair of shoes into
your carry-on for me because no doubt
you'll be looking to borrow them when
we're over there!

ENYA

I didn't even bring a case; I'm going with

the clothes on my back and hoping for a
washing machine in the hotel.

Once your gang makes it through security and everyone breathes
a sigh of relief that nobody was ambushed by an unsuspecting
dildo, your mates will disperse into the Duty Free. Some will go
halves on a litre of Grey Goose, others will go halves on toiletries.
The 3-for-2 in Boots is a life saver! What is it about Irish people?
When we go on holiday, we act like money grows on trees! If we
get a bill in the door that our elecky is going up by 15 cent, all
hell breaks loose, 'Joke of a country, it's gone to bits! No wonder
people are emigrating!', but as soon as we pass through security
in Terminal 1, it's like, 'Forty euro for a full Irish breakfast? No
bother, love, take the fifty you're on your feet all morning!'

You'll all congregate in the Garden Terrace Bar, Dublin airport's
infamous watering hole, soon after, where the routine boomerang
for Instagram is essential! The start of what will be an unforgetta-
ble time together. An airport is the only place in the world where it
is acceptable to drink a double vodka and 7up at 8am in the morning with a full Irish. I've heard it's frowned upon in many countries
if you *don't* drink alcohol with your breakfast. (I couldn't tell you
whichcountries, but Ireland is definitely one of them!)

The organizer friend will arrive first, of course. Holding a
table while the rest linger in the perfume section downstairs.

SARAH

Girls, look at the screen, it's saying final call, go to the gate!

ENYA

Ah will you relax, you've still got a full drink in front of you! We'll be grand. The queue will be a mile long to board, they always have you waiting in the stairwell for ages, like a herd of cattle, and we will be raging we left so early. They won't leave without us.' you can guarantee, 100 per cent, that they will in fact, leave without you. *(Apparently I'm the not-so-punctual friend as well. I genuinely am late to everything, so if the shoe fits!)*

The timekeeper finally gets her wish, and you embark on the long stretch of bollox that is the walkway from Terminal 1 to the gates! And they will almost always send you to the *last* gate in the airport, every time! I call them the skinny gates because by the time you reach them, you've dropped a dress size. It's a walk that only lasts a matter of seconds while heading off on holiday but will most definitely feel like eternity, when you land home! I remember I ran into a group of women all wearing pink shirts one year.

'You all off on a hen do, girls!?'

'No', they sighed, 'we're doing Couch to 5k.'

I love the part when you arrive at your gate, because if you're heading to the Canaries, you will see a wide variety of people boarding the flight, from families, to elderly, to a gang of women your own age. The daggers you get from the OAPs. 'Ugh, a young person, having fun and making noise, glad I was never one of those... I really hope they're not in our hotel.'

And then you have the parents with three kids. I honestly could not imagine a week in the sun with three screaming terrors. I can barely look after myself. They always say, once you have kids, it's not a vacation, it's just relocation. I've never been in the middle of having a great time, and thought to myself, do you know what would make this situation even better? Kids.

When you board the plane the tight friend who didn't reserve their seat with the rest of the group will try to haggle her way with an older gentleman who wants to remain in the seat he paid for. Sandwiched between two of your friends.

But how do you get them to move? This one usually always works:

ENYA

Ah Mister, como on! I'm telling you now,

you'll be delighted you switched in the end, see her there? *Points to Sinead.* Pisses like a racehorse, you better hope she doesn't break the seal, which there's a high probability she will, the plane hasn't even taken off yet and she's already drinking her vodka from a water bottle!

SINEAD

Will you shhh!!

ENYA

And see the other two? *Points to Sarah and Ciara.* Loves a good scrap with a few drinks on them, hate the men, they do, and you'll have nowhere to run when we're up in the air.

SARAH

Omg that's a barefaced lie!'

ENYA

I'm just warning you Mister, is this how you want to start your solo trip to

Alicante? Sandwiched in between Sea
Biscuit and Rocky?

The panic-stricken passenger will gladly vacate to the alternative seat after a threat like this.

Once you step off that plane and the wall of heat hits you, it's essential for one of your group to howl those famous words, 'Oh, girls that heat!' You'll all get guided onto one of those dodgy shuttle buses that are almost always overcrowded, and Pedro drives it like he stole it. You'll hop on the coach that will stop off at every hotel in the continent of Europe before it parks up at yours. You'll always get a rep from the UK on these trips. Overly enthusiastic, cracking shit jokes: 'My name's Sharon and I'll be looking after you this week, if you need anything I'll be floating around your hotel over the next seven days!' and then she'll disappear into the abyss, and you won't see her again until you're going home. 'Did you all enjoy your holiday? Did you find everything ok?' Somebody will always pipe up, usually the loud one in your group. 'Well just as well we did Sharon, because you were nowhere to be bleedin' seen!'

When you finally check in to the hotel with your party, someone in the group will inspect the room with one quick look around and will always have something to say about the condition of it.

ENYA

Who recommended this kip, remind me again?

SARAH

I did, because somebody wouldn't pay the extra few quid for a semi-decent hotel that doesn't have a brothel on the third floor or a weed farm in the basement.

ENYA

I should have done better research, the pool is what had me sold on the website. I should have gave the interiors a look over...

When a group of girls open their suitcases on day one of the holiday, it's as if a clothes bomb has exploded. Miscellaneous clothing everywhere. It resembles the stockroom in a charity shop. And you'll always have one friend who will unpack straight away, stow their shorts, tops and bikinis into the two drawers provided for four people, place their dresses neatly on hangers into the wardrobe, not a crease to be seen. It's usually the same person who was super punctual in the airport. This poor soul will spend the majority of her time in the room trying not to break her neck by stepping over loose sandals, handbags, suitcases, used baby wipes, worn denim shorts, dirty underwear, and empty cans of Pringles.

Which friend are you by the pool?

You'll all descend upon the pool where the holiday has officially commenced. Four thirty-year-old female milk bottles lying there in Penney's bikinis awaiting sunstroke. You had to fight off an older British couple for two sun loungers to share among the four of you.

Pool time is where the flirty/slutty friend gets to work. A middle-aged Spanish bar man serving the booze will always take a liking to one of your friends, and it's usually the flirty/slutty friend. He will make her feel beautiful, like the only girl in Alicante, just to earn that €2 tip. (Until you all go home at the end of the week and he's doing it to the next blonde who rolls in off a flight.)

CIARA

Ah girls, I'm after making a new friend
behind the bar. Felipe is his name; he
gave me a double for the price of a single.
I think he likes me, he's a bit of alright.
He said to mo, 'You are very sexy, you go

to the gym? You have nice body. I tell you
what, you have double because you are so
beautiful.' Girls, I was going red, 'Oh will
you stop, Felipe! I only do walking and
the odd bootcamp class.'

Then you have the friend who only booked the holiday to fry
under the midday sun, lathered in carrot oil, baby oil, zero craic
in the afternoon. Not an ounce of factor to be seen. Air pods in,
true crime podcast on, please do not disturb.

The other friend who only goes on holiday to brag about it on
social media.

SARAH

Will someone take a picture of me?
No, wait, go again.
Ok, take it again but this time from the
waist up.
Ok, try a full-body one again. Actually,
can you-

SINEAD

Ah fuck off you with your pictures...I'm
trying to listen to my audio book.

Or that friend who loves to mingle and will talk to literally anything with a pulse. Usually, an old woman beside your group who is hard of hearing, retired and just wants to sunbathe in peace and not drift off to the sound of a Bluetooth speaker playing Belters Only.

> And where are you from?
> Oh Brighton? Never been.
> We're Irish, IRISH!
> Yeah, from Dublin.
> Over here on a piss-up holiday.
> Away from the kids you know yourself,
> I don't have kids, not for me, *they* all do though.
> Do you have kids?
> No?
> Yeah, you're better off!

7 Things to expect on a first night out.

After everyone has had their showers and applied aloe vera to their third-degree burns, you relax on the balcony with a can of Fanta Lemon in one hand and a pack of Lays crisps in the other (ah, bliss) until you finally peel yourself from the deck chair, 'Right, girls, better start doing me makeup.'

The first thing to expect:

There will always be a friend who forgets to bring anything and everything, or in most cases knew quite well they would be bumming off everyone.

'Girls, can I just have a shot of this curler? I forgot to pack mine.'

'Whose charger is this? You're at 65 per cent, can I just throw mine on to have some battery before we go out? I forgot mine.'

'Who owns this mascara, can I use a bit?'

'Who owns this lovely top? Can I wear it?'

'Can I use this hair spray?'

'Are those knickers on the floor? Are they used? If not, can I wear them?'

Second thing to expect:

For pre drinks, you will have a friend who doesn't know what the words 'single measure' mean. If they pour you a drink it will be 99 per cent pure vodka, 1 per cent cranberry. You will gag.

Third thing to expect:

After everyone has gone to the effort of doing themselves up, you will all need an *iconic* pic for the Insta grid before you leave the hotel room. Some will take longer than others. Your patience will be tested. Only the strong will survive.

Fourth thing to expect:

Before you left the room you all agreed not to fall victim to club reps. Try to avoid eye contact. Always say you're meeting friends somewhere else, however someone will always get sucked in. Usually, the friend who wants to adopt every cat that rubs off their leg when abroad. They will fall under the charm of a London Geezer who can get you a booze package you can't turn down for €15 each – in some corner bar that will be empty and stink of piss and vomit.

Fifth thing to expect:

A friend who has chugged six shots of Mickey Finns will find a podium with a pole in the seediest club on the strip and they will swing from it, and they will hurt themselves. They'll end up in a neck brace for the rest of the holiday, all for a video on the gram. 'Sinead!! Watch this! Get it on video!! Lady Marmalade eat your heart out!!' (Proceeds to do a Martini spin.) But on a positive note, it will make for a great tale during a wedding speech someday.

Sixth thing to expect:

One of your friends will meet the love of their life on the first night of the holiday. They will exchange numbers and text back and forth throughout the week until your FBI friend manages to find him on Instagram one afternoon at the pool, only to discover he's got a fiancé and a young baby. 'Men, they're all slimy bastards, every single one of them!'

Seventh thing to expect:

By the end of the night, you will all without a doubt end up back on the balcony, headfirst into a kebab. Purchased in an establishment that definitely does not meet food health and safety requirements.

Sarah
OMG, nicest kebab ever! Better than sex.

Sinead
You must have had some pretty shit rides so.

The Morning-After Debrief

When the sun breaks through the curtains, everyone is like a corpse, stuck to their bed. There will always be one friend who is the first to rise. They can't sit still; they have to always be moving. They'll usually clean up the remains of the balcony feast from the night before. They've been to the shop and back already, bearing bottles of water for everyone. Their flip flops bashing against the tiles will cause the rest to slowly awake from their slumber.

ENYA

It's 8 o'clock in the morning. How are you up and moving around!? You're on holiday.

SARAH

I'm always up at this time. I'm an early riser!' *(She says as she neatly folds away her dirty clothes into her suitcase.)*

ENYA

Well, since you're up, you can go grab us all sunbeds.

It's 11am and the debrief is about to commence. Ham and cheese toasties all round. Except for those whose hangover is too much to bear. The one who consumed the most alcohol is usually the last to join the party.

Which friend are you at breakfast?

*The **medium rare**, Hungover friend*

SINEAD

Here's trouble now.

The **well done,** Hungover Friend

ENYA

Girls, don't be talking, my head is pounding. I ended up going to that bar next to KFC, with all those English lads.

The **so rare it's still got a pulse,** Hungover friend.

SARAH

I left and went home at one, I actually feel pretty fresh, after I got the sunbeds this morning, I went for a 5k walk along the beach.

SINEAD

What time did you get home at, Enya? It must have been late. I didn't hear you come in.

SARAH

It was 4am, I had to let you in because you forgot your key, no surprise there.

ENYA

Ah, sure you were probably up doing your yoga anyway.

CIARA

I didn't hear a thing, I'd sleep through a
bomb.

*The waiter approaches the table, clearly
struck by the smell of stale alcohol, judging by the look on his face, and asks the
group if they'd like anything to eat.*

SINEAD

I'll get beans on toast please.

SARAH

I'll get the same.

ENYA

I'll get an omelette, please.

WAITER

With what toppings?

ENYA

Codeine. Loads of it. And an orange juice.

WAITER

We don't have ora

ENYA

That's fine, can I just get a gin and 7up.

SARAH

Wtf? It's 11am, Enya!

CIARA

Oh I'd be sick ...

ENYA

I can't wait to die at the pool all day.

SARAH

I thought we were visiting the volcanoes this afternoon?

ENYA

I hope the volcanoes is the name of a cocktail bar, because you better not think I'm going on a hill walk in a pair of crocs and with the world's worst hangover.

SARAH

You literally agreed to it last night.

> ENYA
>
> Well, you'll have to pick it up with drunk me.

> SINEAD
>
> Stop, the both of you. We will go tomorrow.

> ENYA
>
> Has anyone else not had a shite since they got here?

> SARAH
>
> OMG I'm going to the pool to read my Kindle!

The Journey Home

The last day of the holiday is usually when everyone is defeated. Sun stroke, neck braces, extramarital affairs, lost phones, liver transplants. Only the mighty withstand a girls' holiday. You all agreed last night you would take it easy; early flight and all that. That was never going to be the case. 'Will we go for a nice meal and just have one or two?' Famous last words! How well do you know your friends to be confident that it will never just be *one*.

One turned into ten cocktails, five shots and getting a taxi home from a villa party up in the back arse of nowhere with only €5 to all your names. You get back to the hotel at sunrise, everything gets fucked into the case. You've only ninety minutes to make your flight. The OCD friend will worry about the consequences later. This morning in particular is an exception. But of course, someone in the group will always have it worse.

SARAH

I've to go to the zoo with the kids today. Fuck my life.

SINEAD

I'm doing a twelve-hour shift tomorrow from 6am, double fuck my life.

ENYA

I don't know about you, but I'm going home to sleep for a month.
Said with the biggest smug look you've ever seen.

You arrive at the airport running on twenty minutes of sleep that you got in the taxi from the villa to the apartment. The only thing you want is your own bed, a curry and Netflix. You carry the weight of the world on your shoulders through a Spanish airport. Chewing your McDonalds on autopilot. The lights are on, but nobody's home. The wheel is moving, but the hamster is dead. You sit on the plane, AirPods in, eye mask on. Everyone is sick of looking at each other. But if someone offered you another holiday with your mates for free tomorrow – you'd do it all again in a heartbeat. Just after a good night's sleep!!

CHAPTER 6

Navigating a Girls' Night Out

Let us go back to the origins or roots of the girls night out, before we get to our thirties! *Clears throat to mimic David Attenborough*

In the urban jungles of the modern world, amidst the bustling streets, a remarkable social phenomenon emerges: the girls' night out. This ritual, seemingly simple yet rich in social intricacies, traces its origins to the deepest roots of human civilization. In the primordial days of humanity, when tribes roamed the earth in search of sustenance and safety, communal gatherings played a vital role in survival. Women, as the nurturers and caretakers of the tribe, would often band together during the moonlit nights, seeking solace, support, and camaraderie. A Bluetooth speaker would have seriously levelled this up …

Ahem! Anyway … as millennia passed and civilizations flourished, the essence of these gatherings evolved, but remained deeply ingrained in the human psyche. In the modern era, the girls' night out has become a symbol of empowerment, friendship, and liberation. (And also provides great material for a maid-of-honour speech.)

Women converge upon bustling thoroughfares, where laughter and chatter fill the air like birdsong in the dawn chorus. With each step, they shed the burdens of everyday life, embracing the freedom of the night. At bars and cafés, they gather like a pride of lionesses around a watering hole, sharing stories, laughter and secrets. The bonds forged in these moments are as strong as the sinew that binds a pack of wolves. Or like that PVA glue, you'd mess with in primary school (remember gluing your thumb and index finger together and panicking when they wouldn't separate? That shit was lethal.)

Ahem … yet, amidst the revelry, there is an unspoken understanding – a sanctuary where vulnerability is met with empathy, and joy is multiplied through shared experiences.

As the night wanes and the city's pulse slows, the girls' night out reaches its crescendo. They depart, dispersing into the darkness like fireflies in the night sky, their spirits uplifted and hearts full. And straight into a Kebab shop, gerruppp!! (Enya stay in character!)

In the annals of human history, the girls' night out stands as a testament to the enduring power of connection, solidarity, and sisterhood — a celebration of life's joys and a refuge in its trials. It is a phenomenon that showcases the remarkable beauty and resilience of the human spirit ...

... okay, I can't do his voice any longer, or I'll morph into him. My fella had to tell me to stop using his voice in the bedroom, it was killing the mood, ever try talk dirty in received pronunciation? Wouldn't recommend. But you get the drift! In short, the girls' night out goes back to the dawn of time; even Eve left Adam at home while she line-danced around the fire with her girls.

But let's return to the 21st century, and reel in the years to reminisce on how we survived a girls' night out in our youth!

From living rooms to parks

Before reserved tables, heels and split taxi fares, who remembers the teenage girls' night out? Remember being sixteen, in school on a cold Friday afternoon in November, down the back of Geography, wondering whose sitting room was vacant that weekend or whose parents were away, so you'd have a free gaff! Who was organizing the off-license run and how much drink could everyone's €10 pooled together get you? Probably half a tray of WKD or Bacardi Breezer orange, before inflation ruined it. Ah, the simplicity – just chilling in your mate's living room, listening to the music channels on a Friday or Saturday night.

Being a teenager meant your parents were obliged to give you some pocket money to allow you to have a social life and get you out of their hair for a few hours, but it came at the cost of washing dishes or hoovering the stairs for the week. I wish I could get my mother or father to fund my Friday / Saturday nights with my mates now!

We were seriously talented at stretching €10 weekly pocket money; I spend €10 on coffee and a protein bar daily nowadays! I spend a minimum of €100 on a night out at the age of thirty, but back then I bled that €10 dry for the whole weekend. How the fuck did we do it? I guess we had to work with what we had. And we had no responsibilities, no overheads, bills or rent. The only expenses we had to worry about were drinking money and lunch money for school that week (but often our mother or father took care of that, so I suppose making our money stretch was the only stressor). If you were really skint, you probably had one mate who always got a bit extra off their parents (the friend who had a mobile in Courtown, Wexford); they'd loan you €10, and you'd pay it back in instalments over the month a bit like the credit union or Klarna. Lifesavers!

We didn't know how good we had it – youth on our side, and non-existent hangovers. Nothing to get up for on Sunday morning, and breakfast and Sunday dinner would be handed to us. We'd lie around all day watching MTV or Nickelodeon until we had to study last minute for the math test on Monday morning or do the rake of homework we promised ourselves we'd do Friday after school. We'd overhear your parents ordering a takeaway and you'd dash down the stairs in your Penny's PJs to bum a free plate of chicken curry off them.

In my friend group we had one mate whose living room was always vacant on the weekend. She didn't have a regular mom; she had a 'cool mom' (did you catch that *Mean Girls* reference?) Her mother would go upstairs while we occupied downstairs. Her mam pretended she didn't know what we were up to, but she was well aware. There was no way six teenage girls were confidently belting out Rihanna's 'Umbrella', sounding like a bag of cats being lambasted against a wall, under the influence of Fanta and Coke. One girl would be in charge of the remote/DJ, one girl would be responsible for refills, one girl in charge of being zero craic because she was playing text tennis with her fella on her pink Motorola razor phone (she would eventually leave early to give him the shift on a nearby street corner.) There was one girl responsible for buzzing the curry shop, where we'd get the cheapest thing on the menu just for the sake of being able to order food. This was before we counted calories or knew what a gym was.

There was another friend in charge of the digital camera. She'd take two hundred candid photos of us all parading around a bottle of cheap vodka like an Oscar trophy or Simba from *The Lion King*. Those pictures would be uploaded straight to Bebo the following morning via a usb cable and a Dell laptop. We all thought we were such rebels, going back into school on Monday broadcasting how much craic it was, 'Ah you missed it, it was the funniest.' Bragging about how much we drank, what fellas were itching to come round. Bouncing around the sitting room in our fluffy socks till 1am until someone got sick and the party was swiftly over.

If you had a mate with a shed out their back garden, it felt like you had won the friend lottery! Jackpot! Like Sally with the biscuits! Spot sorted till we turn eighteen! Bonus points if their parents had their own mini bar, you'd empty the bottles of vodka and replace them with water. Double bonus points if they had a side entrance and you didn't have to face their parents on the way out at the end of the night, or even worse, the next morning. It's funny how the tables turn back again; I'd much rather drink in a sitting room or shed now at thirty than be out in any club or pub.

Then summer rolled around, and the temperature was warm enough to migrate from your mate's sitting room and into the parks. It was all about gathering up the troops – twenty or thirty like-minded sixteen-year-olds from the area. Using someone for their battery-operated speakers (no such thing as Bluetooth, it was an Aux cable or nothing.) Walking through the local estates full of glee and mischief, everyone carrying a plastic bag full of alcopops, trying to drown out the bottles clinking with laughter and chatter so your neighbours wouldn't look out their window and rat to one of the parents. The six-for-a-tenner deal that some dodgy aul fella got for you in the local off license if you paid for his smokes. Fashion wasn't a concern. Nobody knew what 'jeans and a nice top' was, there was no *pretty little thing* or *boohoo* – no online shopping for that matter. People knew what was in style through magazines they read in a dentist's waiting room or in the local hairdressers. Back then it was Airmax, and your freshest Lacoste tracksuit, gold hoops you robbed on your ma or older sister, and a good spray of Britney Spears Fantasy.

There was always that one freak in the group who opened bottles with their teeth, because you would always forget to bring along the bottle opener. Someone had *one* job! Rob the Lanzarote magnet from their parents' fridge and bring it to the park! I wonder where those heroes are now who risked their canines for us, probably on a flight home from Turkey with a new set of delf! Everyone was assigned a job, there was a girl on lookout duty, making sure the gardaí didn't spot us; if they did, we didn't walk, we *ran*!

As far as my mother knew I was at a friend's sleepover eating a homemade pizza with her family watching *Winning Streak*, not in the middle of a field sculling drink with girls and lads from the area. Another mate was on DJ duty, they were lucky enough to own an iPod with all the latest tunes on it (they were also the same friend who loaned you the €10). We all sat in a semi-circle on freshly cut grass on a Saturday evening mid-summer, blaring Akon's greatest hits without a care in the world. But what if one of us needs to go to the toilet – we can't go home stinking of drink? That's when another job was assigned, someone kept the lookout for dog walkers while you squatted and pissed in a bush. Men have it so easy. Ah, the glamour of teenage drinking. Although some of those bushes were a lot more glamorous than some of the pub or club cubicles I've been in over the years.

The in-between, or priming stage before the glory years began

Before we eventually became of legal age and progressed to nightclubs, we were softly broken in with underage discos. Some of these were wild. This is where girls slowly began to become conscious of our appearance, and show interest in fashion (or what we thought was fashion.) We began to transition out of the tracksuits. I cringe when I think back to some of the outfits. How I garnered any male attention in these getups I'll never know. We would meet in my friend's bedroom (the friend who had parents who could afford to clothe their child regularly) and we pull her wardrobe apart – crop tops, shorts, skirts, dolly shoes and fake gold jewellery. Going into school on Monday with a prominent green ring around your neck howled council estate. We would proceed to raid my friend's makeup drawer. If anybody remembers foundation mousse and Sunshimmer fake tan, you were one of my comrades and I salute you. We were the guinea pigs for false tan in its infancy. Thankfully it's come on leaps and bounds since the early noughties, but I bet you can still smell it. We hadn't a clue how to blend our neck and face together, the divide was so apparent it was like night and day, and I would have so much eyeliner on, I resembled an Irish Cleopatra. (Or *Cleeooo* for short, because I'm from Dublin.) There was no such thing as stick-on lashes back in those days, you'd have to cake your lashes in mascara. Between the eye liner, mascara and unblended smoky eye – no YouTube tutorials or make-up artists (MUAs) back then either – we looked like we'd face planted a fireplace, but we thought we were only stun hun.

My friend's dad would drop us to the door of the event,

because we didn't have the luxury of affording our own transport. He would give us a lecture about no hands below the belt. I didn't understand it at the time, but now I do, and I recoil. The discos would be in a local community hall, girls on one side, boys on the other and you'd meet in the middle and hope for the best. Everyone was strung out on TK Red Lemonade and Burger Bite crisps. Someone would find a way to sneak in a naggin (it wasn't hard to tell who it was, they'd be the only one violently vomiting in the toilets or out front.) There was always a girl in the group who caught every boy's attention and you'd have to be the wing girl for his mate during a slow set, and he'd never be gifted in the looks, brains or fashion department. But who am I to judge. Do they still do slow sets at teenage discos? They definitely don't do them in clubs or pubs – bring back the slow sets!!

Side note: even in your thirties you'll still have a friend who will catch every man's eye, but she's just got better at telling them, 'Piss off! I'm engaged!'

Then eventually came the time where the oldest friend in the group would turn eighteen, they'd go to their first nightclub with their older sister and her friends, and they'd tell you all about it in school on the Monday. People would gather around them before the class started, they were like a prophet, you'd be hurling questions at them, what was it like? What was the music like? What were the lads like? How late did you stay out? How much were the drinks? How far would €10 get you!? You'd be livid with jealousy, but also curious, because you knew your turn would soon come. That's if you weren't already using a fake ID and had to memorize your cousin's friend's sister's date of birth and star sign.

I'll never forget the first time I stepped into a nightclub. I'm the oldest out of my friend group, so I had to wait for the next person to turn eighteen before I had anyone to go out with. I was in the local pub with my friend one Friday evening. We knew two lads who were heading the local nightclub. We decided to go at the last minute, because why not? I was young and I had no work to get up for. I was in a pair of UGG boots – yes *UGG* boots – with jeans and a cardigan and not a screed of makeup on. We had €30 between us, a whole €5 increase from the usual €10, we were coming up in the world. Joke, I was still stretching money from my birthday. We got two drinks each, stood on the outskirts of the dance floor and took it all in, one Nicki Minaj song at a time. The fashion, the etiquette, the lads, the maturity, a far cry from the community halls; a whole new world was upon us.

Adultescence

Some years have passed, you're all in college and now in your early twenties. Mammy and Daddy have forced you out into the world of work because your social life began to cause some financial strain on their pocket. A job to fund your wardrobe, your weekends, your transport to and from college and your takeaways or Eddie Rocket dates with the girls – and also your credit union loan. This is where you transition into Miss Independence and get a taste of the big, bold world of responsibilities. You're still a spring chicken, but this time around you've got more cash to line your pockets. Instead of spending your only €10 on six bottles of VK from Lidl, to sit in your mate's sitting room and listen to the best of Hip-Hop & R'n'B, you've now got about €30 to spare, so the options were endless!

When you're in your early twenties, being able to go to nightclubs on the weekend with a valid and legit ID was revolutionary and a privilege. It was what everyone did at the time. It was a phase of life. If you weren't out in a club on the weekend, you weren't cool. Nobody went to pubs; they were for *old* people. Let me take you down memory lane and explain how a typical night out in your twenties should go.

Nights out in your twenties

- The *night out* is established at the weekly board meeting. If you had a friend who could drive in the group, you had once again hit the friend lottery! My friends and I actually christened our driver friend 'Micra.' This little washing machine of a car is where the board meeting took place and where weekend plans were venue-decided, usually based on what was the local hotspot at the time, but also where had the best drink promotions. I'll always remember the specials in my local nightclub: €10 for a double Captain Morgans and Fanta orange. That would be worth about €15 - €18 now! And by God did we make that last the night, especially if we wanted to afford a Big Mac at home time. We'd also decide the day, the time, the outfits, whose shoes we'd borrow, handbags, how much money would be needed, whose house would be most suitable for pre-drinks.

• Saturday rolls around and you all meet at 'Micra's' house for pre drinks. If you only had €30 to spare for a taxi to and from the venue, drinks at the venue and food afterwards, you made sure you got pre drinks in. At the ripe age of twenty-one, it was all about cost efficiency and the game changer was buying a small naggin of vodka worth about €10, to sneak into the venue. A mixer would only cost about €3, you'd be saving about €4 on the vodka shot, which meant you could garner more drinks. The friend with the naggin was usually the one who didn't have a job yet, but wanted the best of both worlds. Walking up to the entrance of the venue, awaiting your fate, hoping the bouncer wouldn't check your clutch bag is what I imagine it's like to walk through customs with two thousand cigarettes in your case for the purpose of 'personal use'. Those types of friends would go out with €10 in their pocket, get pissed, get food on the way home and still wake up with change to spare. In later years they would go on to appear on TV shows such as *Extreme Cheapskates* and *Benefit Street*. Definition of Champagne lifestyle on a lemonade wage!

- You'd show up to your mates for pres in the shortest, skimpiest dress on the rack, and you'd spend most of the night pulling the dress down over your arse because the lycra keeps riding up on you. You didn't wear heels, you wore stilts. You were like Bambi on ice. Flat shoes were out of the question, they were something your ma or aunt wore. No tables to sit at in the venue? No problem, our feet are still young and recover quickly. Blisters from dancing all night? Never heard of them.

- Make up had progressed slightly as you could afford better drugstore products, but you still weren't skilled in the eye shadow appliance department. Yes you learned how to blend your foundation a bit better, but I bet you look back on old photos now and think to yourself, *Who the fuck let me leave the house with a black-cut crease?* If you lacked any products, Micra would usually have a stash that people sponged from. It was like a salon wholesalers in her room, hairspray, perfume, deodorant, tan, lipstick.

- Once the taxi was *en route*, everyone was ordered to congre gate in the kitchen for a group photo, to prove to social media the night out actually happened. Think of all the crap you put into your clutch bag for a night out in this day and age. Now imagine the weight of a digital camera as well as your phone. Camera phones back in 2010 were atrocious, the digital camera was your only chance of getting a clear photo of your night out.

- I would like to take this opportunity to apologize to any taxi men who were unfortunate enough to transport me and my friends to or from the club many years ago. We were like feral animals. It's like we were never let out before. Loud and obnoxious and God forbid Whitney Houston came on the radio. 'Mr Taxi Driver! Will you higher that up!!' We would sing so badly we'd have the power to shatter windows and scare away small animals.

- As you exited the taxi, there was always one friend who never had any change, 'Micra will you grab my fare and I'll get you a drink in there?' This is coming from the same girl who brought a naggin with her to avoid buying **any** alcohol. (*How do you approach a problem like this? You say to them, 'I'll walk you to the bar right now, Mary, can get me a bottle of WKD with a straw, please. Break that €10 note that's sticking out of your fake Gucci purse, and we will make sure you have change for the taxi home.' You have to be firm and assertive, because otherwise they* *will disappear into the abyss, and you won't see them for the rest of the night. They're usually the types that disappear when it's their turn to buy a round as well. #NoShame #YouKnowWhoYouAre)*

- In your twenties you could dance all night, fall into a taxi, force the taxi driver to go through McDonald's Drive-thru for a euro-saver hamburger, devour it before you got home. Fall into bed at two am. Wake up at 8am feeling a little dishevelled, saunter into work on a Sunday at 9am with last night's make-up still on your face and the nightclub wristband still wrapped around your wrist, ready to take on your 8-hour shift in Dunnes Stores. All of the above dramatically changes after 30. DRAMATICALLY.

Nights out after the age of thirty

Nights out are rare at this age, and usually you only congregate with your pals if it's a special occasion, otherwise you're going to need to give the WhatsApp group at least three months' notice. And Good luck getting everyone to agree on the same date.

I'm away with the kids that weekend.

I've a wedding that day.

I've a work night out that night.

My babysitter's away that weekend.

We're saving for a mortgage so count me out.

I'm pregnant.

I'm home for Christmas, we will have to catch up then.

- When you *finally* agree on a date that suits everyone, then the disputes start over the location of the night out.

Ah, that's a shit hole, always trouble there.

They don't sell wine, I just checked.

They don't sell food either, how are we meant to line our stomachs?

My sister was spiked there last year.

It's a bit far for me.

Bouncers are pricks on there.

Nightmare getting a taxi out of there.

- Pre-drinks are a thing of the past and now that you've all got a nice chunk of disposable income, everyone can afford their own taxi.

I'm working late, I'll meet you all there.

Baby won't settle, I'll be an hour late.

I'll get him to drop me in, still not ready.

Still waiting to get a blow dry, running late also.

- There is no such thing as clothes swapping anymore. You're now in a position where you buy a new outfit for every night out. God forbid there were pictures circulating of you wearing the same dress twice. If twenty-year-old Enya could see me now! Kiss goodbye to heels, they only come out if there's a wedding. Boots or flats are your only option. Comfort is key now. You've been traumatized enough over the years, and still carry the battle wounds from walking miles in stilettos to pull a taxi during the Christmas period. You learned the hard way.

- Gone are the days you'd sneak a naggin in and stretch €10 for the night. It's rounds of cocktails and sharing bottles of house wine these days.

- Then when you get to the bar, *not* nightclub because you've outgrown them by now. That's when the horror sets in.

There are no tables!? Did nobody reserve one!? Where are we supposed to sit? I'm not standing in these shoes all night!

It's full of kids in here. I used to babysit her over there.

That music is very loud; I can't hear myself think.

Is that girl not freezing in that dress? How is she walking in them heels?

I'm not mad about that DJ; would he not play a bit of Take That?

Girls, we should leave before last orders to beat the taxi queues.

I can only stay till midnight because I'm up with the kids in the morning.

- Getting home you usually disperse into separate taxis; you've spent enough time around these people for one night. On the rare occasion someone's hubby or boyfriend would be stung with giving you all a lift home. He'd have to hear all about the night's antics. He might have to pull over once or twice while someone regurgitates their single shot of sambuca on the side of the dual carriage way. You'd get pleasure in reminding them, 'You can't drink like you used to!'

- Stopping for food is also not an option, especially if you have kids. You're eating into sleep time. Sleep is precious. You'd have a nice Solpadeine and electrolyte cocktail waiting by your bedside to minimize hangover damage. After thirty the hangovers take 3 - 5 working days to leave your system.

Types of friends on a night out

The networker: The friend who mingles mostly in the smoking area, not only to bum free smokes, but to cling on to a set of lads in the hopes of a free drink or after-party. Don't rely on sticking with these folk on a night out; they're free spirits, say your goodbyes when you enter the building because they've no intention of sticking with the group

The one who can't handle their drink: There's one in every group – alcohol just doesn't agree with them. They chug the bottles and shots too soon, until they're crammed into a cubicle screaming 'Hewweeyy' into the toilet bowl and some poor unfortunate stuck holding their clip in-hair extensions out of their face, 'Where's all the carrots coming from!? You didn't even eat carrots today!' I would advise warning them during pre-drinks about what they're capable of, but they always swear, 'No, not tonight! I'm pacing myself.' And then they get there and do the exact opposite. You're talking to a wall, but unfortunately someone has to babysit them. I'd recommend a game of rock-paper-scissors in the group to settle it.

Agony Aunt: She lingers in the bathroom for most of the night, telling broken-hearted younger women how they 'don't need no man to make them happy, happiness starts from within, you've your whole life ahead of you! Don't make the same mistakes I did, separated, with two kids and a mortgage. Now, turn that phone off, wipe your tears and go upstairs and up end that dance floor!'

Years down the line, she will probably go on to be this woman's bridesmaid. Women like this thrive in these environments; let them spread their wings among the sisterhood, female power and all that. It's their gift to give, what they were born to do, like a female Martin Luther King, except their stage is in some dingy toilet that stinks of urine and hair spray. They usually set up a podcast down the line. And these women always have the best stories in the taxi home. 'Girls, wait til I tell you what happened in the jacks tonight.'

The trouble riser: Craves a scrap. They can't wait for someone to stumble into them, and before you know it, a girl gets pushed into another girl and all hell breaks loose, heels and earrings are flying. The bouncers rush in to break it up. '*She* fuckin started it!!' (She definitely *wasn't* the one who started it!) The best thing you can do is be on standby with a trench coat, throw it over her like Kevin Costner in *The Bodyguard*, and get Whitney out of there!

The one who keeps buying shots for everyone: In your youth you had a gag reflex of steel. I remember in my early twenties I would often chug three Jagerbombs in a row on a Saturday night, like water off a duck's back. If I even smell one now, I'm green. If you have a friend like this, don't try to rebel, it never works, just throw it over your shoulder when she's not looking.

The pretty girl: This friend evaluates how good of a night she had based on how many lads interacted with her. If she caught a good one, that's it, you could be bleeding to death on the floor in front of her and she will not be fazed by you. You no longer exist, goodbye. These friends are zero craic. They even get warned before you go out. 'Now, it's a girls' night tonight, Sarah. Don't be going off with fellas and disappearing like usual.' Leave them be, they're the ones missing out on the memories.

The one who minds all the clutch bags while everyone is off fulfilling their duties: These friends don't smoke, don't mingle with lads and are very introverted. They were led to believe everyone would stay at the same table for the entire night and swap stories as if sitting around a campfire. Rookie mistake! With age they will learn to just stay at home and enjoy a bottle of wine.

The 'Irish goodbye' friend: These have just had enough! Too drunk to care and too tired to face the *Don't go home!* committee. 'Ah, stay! We're all going in a minute anyway, the night's nearly over, have one more!' They are more common in groups after the age of thirty. When you were younger you couldn't afford to get a taxi by yourself, you'd have to hang around until the lights came on and the horrendous taxi queues would commence. I'm a sucker for an Irish goodbye; I don't even say goodbye, I just say I'm going the loo and never return. Drop them all a text when I'm back in bed. What can they do then?

Getting older and drifting apart from your friends is inevitable, but it's who you grow old with that matters. Are your mates willing to pawn the kids off with their dad or grandparents, or miss work on Monday for one mad night of the year? Life does get in the way and nights out are few and far between, but age is only a number when it comes to having fun! You're never too old for a wild night out. Just ask me nanny. It's funny how one day you're necking Jaeger bombs and still jumping up out of bed for a 9am shift the following morning, and the next you're drinking water in between each drink and waking up in critical condition.

CHAPTER 7

Surviving a Hen Party

So, you've been summoned to a hen party? My heart breaks for you. I've had my fair share of them, so let me elaborate on what to expect and how to survive one – especially if it's a bad one! You know what I'm talking about don't you? The hen party you would be delighted NOT to be invited to (though you' be disgusted NOT to be invited to the wedding.) I've gone to hen parties that were some of the best weekends of my life, and I've been to hen parties that were so boring I wanted to get up in the middle of the night and do an Irish goodbye back to Dublin.

There are two types of hen parties you will encounter in life and they both have their pros and cons. They are as follows:

The boring type

You have to go because the bride or groom are an immediate family member or whatever.

The bridal party thinks they're mad bitches, but they're *not* actually mad bitches. Everyone at the hen is from a normal functioning family, the craic is far from mighty, more like contained and organised.

You'll usually be invited via email, as the maid of honour is OCD, takes her job very seriously and has a degree in Event and Operations Management. She was that kid in school who would remind the teacher at the end of a school day, 'Miss! You forgot to give us our homework!' You'll be prompted to fill out a Google form.

- Are you available on these dates?
- What size are you in a t-shirt? I know the manager of Brown Thomas and we can get good quality black t-shirts for €80–€100.
- Have you got any allergies – where are all my gluten intolerant girls at?
- History of heart disease?
- How many points did you get in the Leaving Cert?
- What college did you go to Trinity, UCD or DCU?
- Are you with VHI?

- Have you got an island in your kitchen or a downstairs toilet?

Then once the screening form is out of the way, the WhatsApp group is established.

- WhatsApp group set up 0.5 seconds later by maid of honour (Note: she hasn't even been elected maid of honour yet, this is totally based on assumption).
- Intro message from smug maid of honour:

> Hi, everyone! I know what you're thinking: 'Ugh, not another WhatsApp group!' I promise it won't be one of those groups that ping every 10 seconds (*it will be*). I'll keep it short and sweet; my name is Dearbhla and I'm the maid of honour, eeek! So excited to meet you all. Catherine passed on all your numbers, so I thought it would be easier to add you all into the hen party group so we can throw out suggestions on where to go. Catherine would like to go away on August bank holiday, and according to the Google Form you all filled out, it seems you're all free. Catherine said her nan is coming along too, so nowhere too mad, lol.

- Next stage: Multiple suggestions on where to go and also multiple objections. Which go something like this: 'I wouldn't be mad on going to Liverpool, my next-door neighbour's dog walker, knew a guy, whose girlfriend went to Liverpool and got mugged!!

- (Corporate Sally) replied: Hi, Dearbhla, I hope this message finds you well. So excited. I'll go anywhere once there's Wi-Fi and coffee, but if we could avoid anywhere close to a council estate that would be ideal as peasants give me the ick!

Expect daily messages chasing up t-shirt money and hotel-room splits.

> Hi ladies, I hate to be a pest, but twelve people (*the whole group*) still haven't sent money for t-shirts or rooms. This is going to be a really fun weekend and I would hate for any lady to miss out because of poor time and financial management. If any lady is having financial difficulties, could you text me offside, so I can invite someone else instead #peasants :)

So, the group decides on the Cliffs of Moher (a remote location, couldn't be further from a council estate if they tried), as the bride would like to do a wholesome trip for two nights because

Nanny loves the west of Ireland, and we can't bring Nanny to Liverpool. So, we've settled on a 'Hens in the Irish Countryside'. You've probably gathered that these are the type of women that will go to the local pub in Clare, do two shots of Sambuca at the bar with a wedding veil around their heads, and claim it's still to this day, one of the maddest nights of their life. You were in bed by 11pm, calm down, Dearbhla, before someone gets arrested.

A few characters you'll expect to meet on a hen party like this:

Nanny

She doesn't know it's a hen and was led to believe it was a holy trip to Knock. Considering the group of women who are going, she probably won't even notice the difference.

The Cousin - Corporate Sally

Never switches off from work, brings a laptop everywhere.

The Maid of Honour – Dearbhla

Bestie with the bride since their time in boarding school.

The Bride – Catherine

Met her husband Fintan in Croker after Ireland won the Six Nations. She got free tickets to a corporate box, as she's an 'Influencer.' She will vlog the whole hen trip, pretending that she's enjoying herself when in reality, she's delaying every event on the itinerary because she takes 100 million photos for her Instagram, and ends up picking the first one that she took. But won't get in anyone's photos or videos without her approval in case it damages her 'brand identity'.

The Mother-in-Law – Patricia

Would have preferred everyone to enjoy drinks and a BBQ out in her back garden , any excuse for a group of women to stroke her ego about her remodelled patio. And also another opportunity to whip out the photo albums and ramble on how the sun shines out of her son's arse. She loves to brag.

The bulk of women at these types of hen parties are very corporate, prim and proper, they let their job consume them. They are allergic to carnage, it disgusts them. That's how they get pissed so quickly after two shots of Mickey Finns. That's when corporate Sally isn't so corporate anymore, so she's learned to rein in her drinking since she got promoted to Account Director at her advertising firm. They'll wave around a plastic willy in the pub, *once the nanny has her back turned*, but probably haven't seen a real one in years. These women enjoy a glass of wine at home, in one of those expensive cauldron-like glasses, before bed, while watching *The Great British Bake Off.* The type that set up an Instagram page for their dog because they think other people idolise their pooch as much as they do. *WE DON'T.* They operate Excel sheets in their sleep. They get up at 6am to go to the gym, count their macros, and love avocado on toast with their morning coffee.

Activities to expect on a weekend full of wannabe mad, but secretly corporate, bitches:

☑ **Itinerary:** (printed out and laminated in A6 size, attached to lanyard to wear around neck for the weekend)

Day one

☐ **9am sharp** – Arrive at cliffs of Moher Manor

☐ **10am** – Afternoon tea in the foyer / followed by mini photoshoot for Catherine's Instagram.

☐ **12pm** – *Sound of Music* themed hill walk, and everyone has to dress up as a member of the Von Trapp family. Catherine already chose Julie Andrews, sorry to disappoint.

☐ **2pm** – Recreational or chill time, as nan needs her afternoon nap after she's airlifted from the cliffs.

☐ **3pm** – Meet in the foyer to help Catherine with a sponsored TikTok video, we need two extras, someone to hold a ring light, and someone to operate the mics.

☐ **4pm – 5pm** – Wine tasting – limit to one glass per person – don't want to overdo it. No videos of Catherine tasting wine, it might damage her relationship with brands.

☐ **6pm** – Everybody meets in the foyer for dinner, taxi pick up to bring us to the most expensive restaurant in the country, according to the *Irish Times*. Catherine was offered a free meal, if she gives a shout out to the restaurant on her Instagram.

☐ **8pm** – Drinks are optional – don't want to overdo it as we're up for kayaking in the morning. Catherine has a curly blow dry booked at 9am so she won't be kayaking, but she will be sitting in a kayak temporarily for photos, purely for a social media post.

Day two

☐ **8am** – Yoga

☐ **10am** – Kayaking

☐ **12pm** – Lunch in the hotel courtyard – I've requested to have the hotel harpist join us for some ambient music.

☐ **1pm** – Catherine's Glam Squad arrives on site for the big night out!

☐ **3pm** – Manicure & pedicure, this one is on Catherine, how kind! (You'll still have to pay but if you use her discount code, you'll get 10 per cent off)

☐ **6pm** – Photoshoot in Catherine's suite, she's requested you don't outshine her outfit or make-up so please show up looking like a melted welly, if possible. Everyone wears black. Catherine to wear white. While we're on the subject of clothes, can we send Catherine pictures of our outfits to make sure nobody wears a similar outfit to Catherine over the weekend. If that does happen, there's a Penney's 100 kilometres away :)

☐ **8pm** – Visit a local pub, limit to 3 drinks per person – as we're up at 6am for a 5k run. Catherine is working with a charity that feeds people and supports their basic needs, and she's doing a 5k run for them. This was the only weekend she could fit it in, so if everyone could bring €10 for a donation, that would be great. (The charity is called 'Influencers who have less than 10,000 followers but are trying to make money from it.')

☐ **11pm** – Bed, skincare routine, lights out, phones off, Wi–Fi off, doors locked. You can't escape.

Pros of such a hen party:

- You won't have to book the Monday off work.
- You won't realize how strong you were until being strong was your only option
- Kid friendly

Cons:

- Three days of your life you'll never get back.

- Zero craic

- No good tales to tell years down the line.

- If this is how shit the hen is, imagine the wedding weekend.

- Twelve more Facebook friends you didn't need.

Excuses you can use to not attend such a hen party - thank me later!

- I have COVID. This one will never get old. You can use it for anything really! It's the ultimate cop out. When *Busted* went to the year 3000, they said, 'Not much has changed but people are still getting COVID.'

- 'I couldn't get it off work, someone is on holiday the same weekend.' Nobody can argue with this! You might not even have a job, how are they to know!

- 'I've a colonoscopy booked for the same weekend.' Nobody is going to question that, nor want you to go into more detail.

- 'The hen party is way out of my budget at the moment' - you can't really argue with that, if you're broke, you're broke. However, be careful of what you post on socials for the weeks that follow, for example, don't advertise your shiny, new black Mercedes E-class when you were crying poverty two weeks ago.

- You had a fling with the groom many moons ago - Probably steer clear of this one if the groom is your brother. Or maybe your family is into that shit. I'm not one to judge. Each to their own.

- If you really want to be honest, you could just say 'No thanks, bride is a C**T', and just exit the WhatsApp group.

Now, let's talk about a WIILLLLLD hen party weekend:

We've covered the violently boring hen party, let's get to the wild one, my favourite! Although they *do* come with their own set of pros and cons. The bulk of women at these types of hen parties are from dysfunctional families. Most of the girls going have been friends with the bride 'since we were in nappies together'. These are the *real* mad bitches. Sick of the fella and the kids, can't wait to piss off for three days and get shitfaced, any type of escape from reality, phone on airplane mode the minute they hit the airport, do not disturb. Doesn't matter where it is. Their attitude is, it's not where you go, it's who you go with! But 90 per cent of the time it's Benidorm. A location like Benidorm is a lighthouse for women like this.

The WhatsApp group was set up seconds after the engagement announcement on Facebook and Instagram. The group will probably be called something like 'Sluts on tour'. Nobody gives a shit that their friend is about to embark on this beautiful new chapter with the love of her life, they're all just thinking of the drinking opportunities it provides.

177

Stacey sets up group 'Sluts on tour'.

Stacy

Yup girls! What's the craic? Stacey here, Sarah's bestie. I know most of yas know me from Sarah's 30th, yeah that was me who belly flopped off a table onto the dance floor. Rib cage still in bits, but we live and learn. So, my girl is getting married! Can't believe she'll never ride anyone else again! Devo! Ah no I'm messing, I love Tomo. I know the wedding is going to be fab and all, but can we talk about how mad the hen is going to be!? I'm living for it; I'm pissed just thinking about it! I was born to organize this. So, what are we thinking? Beni or Liverpool? And the t-shirts... I know a fella who prints them and gets the shirts off the back of a truck. He said he will do us a deal for €10 apiece. You can drop the cash into me, don't want the social seeing money going through me bank or Revolut, you know yourself.

Craig

I'll go anywhere once there's sun and cocktails, up to me neck with the credit union for this bleerin hens, but f**k it, anything for me pal Sarah.

Michelle

First time away from the kids for more than 24 hours, nervous, but also excited!

Stacey

Is your eldest not 16 years of age, Michelle!? How the f**k have you not been away in 16 years?

Mother-in-Law, Bernie

What's a Revolut?? Thanks Stacey, looking forward to this.

A few characters you'll expect to meet on a hen party like this:

Bride - Sarah - hairdresser

Met her fella, 'Tomo the electrician', on a night out after years of dating walking red flags. Kissed him in the smoking area and the rest was history.

Maid of honour - Stacey - Lash technician

She's still single. She's been there for Sarah through all the break ups, been sleepover buddies throughout all their teenage years, had their first smoke together. You don't cross Stacey, she'll go through you for a shortcut. Classic resting bitch face persona.

Michelle – Bridesmaid – The responsible friend who is married

Used to be the mental bitch of the group years ago before she settled down with the hubby and three kids. Her family is her life, so she's anxious the whole weekend. She has serious trust issues that her husband won't be able to keep her kids alive for seventy-two hours. Frequent phone calls throughout the day, multiple Facetime calls during activities, feels guilty for getting too drunk because she'll be paying for it for the week and her time with her kids will suffer. Proper Mammy.

Married women warning These are the type of women who have been locked up for so long, in mammy mode, they become institutionalized. When they are released back into the wild, it's like a criminal being released from prison after serving life. Once they taste the alcohol and hear the Venga boys pumping from the nightclub sound system it's like they are eighteen again. It's game over. They become a liability. I recommend putting an air tag in their pocket because they will 100 per cent go missing and God knows for how long. But you can always count on them to turn up to the airport when you're heading home, just about in one piece.

The gay best friend - Craig - unemployed - chronic smoker

Got a credit union loan to go on this trip – will be the only male at the hen party and couldn't care less, he's here for a good time not a long time. According to him, there can never be enough willy straws. He will 100 per cent make Sarah walk around the airport with a naked blow-up doll and plant a rubber willy and a bottle of liquid in her carry-on suitcase, so she's pulled at security.

The weird cousin that nobody knows – Siobhan

There's always one of these at every hen party, usually sitting on Nanny's lap the whole weekend. They don't speak to anyone the entire weekend, just occasionally show up in the background of activities. The only reason she's there is because the bride is an immediate family member. This is her worst nightmare; she'd rather be at home reading *Harry Potter* for the 150th time.

Mother-in-law – Bernie

Picture the most wholesome woman you know, now multiply her by ten. That's Bernie in a nutshell! Still attends mass on a Sunday morning, cuts her grass religiously and never forgets anyone's birthday. Always the first to comment on a new profile picture, 'Absolutely fabulous, hun!' But the moment she sets foot on that minibus and gets a jelly shot into her – it's like a spell takes over her and she's no longer Sister Bernie, she's all about willies, will literally become *aggressively* obsessed with willies. Any chance she gets, she'll turn something into a sexual innuendo.

Example: Group at breakfast in hotel one morning

WAITER

Can I take your order, ladies?

BERNIE

Have you got a big, thick black pudding, not the sliced pudding I just want a big, black, long one?

WAITER

Ermm I can che—

BERNIE

If you don't, would you have those big, thick jumbo sausages? You know the ones you do nearly choke on?

CRAIG

Oh, I'll have them too, if there's any going!

The women at these types of hen parties behave like feral cats or dogs. Absolutely no shame, will have vodka in their cornflakes, at the breakfast buffet 'F**k it, it's 5 o'clock somewhere girls!' Some of them only running on two hours of sleep beause they haggled the barman to keep the resident bar open until 4am instead of. Would turn the local karaoke bar, which resembled Larry Masseys, into a full-blown live Abba concert. People up on their feet cheering for more. Stacey up on podium in the local nightclub, swinging from poles. Bernie is also swinging from a pole, imagining it's something else. Craig up on stage singing with the drag queens, Stacey has to be carried home, because her ten-inch heels have her feet crippled. Michelle on Facetime to her kids in the women's toilets. Cousin Siobhan carted off in an ambulance because she got a rubber willy to the side of the head. All you can do is hope you're sharing a room with a person of sound mind. And that's just on night one!

Itinerary one might expect a hen party like this

☑ A screenshot from Stacey's notes app sent into the WhatsApp group. It's up to you to download the picture and know the chain of events for over the weekend in Benidorm.

Day one

☐ **10am** – Airport pick up – Minibus booked - Bring your own cans.

☐ **10:30 am** – Arrive at Dublin airport.

☐ **10:45pm** – Get through security.

☐ **11am** – Get pissed in Garden Terrace Bar.

☐ **8pm** – Flight to Benidorm. Some of us aren't sitting with the group, but if there's a stranger beside us and they refuse to move, I'll skull drag them up and down the aisle until they do.

In the event the flight is delayed, I've contacted Terminal 2, their bar opens until 1am. Sorted.

☐ **11pm** – Arrive in Alicante

☐ **11:30 pm** – Taxi drop-off to hotel. Bags dropped in room, straight out onto strip, no time for pictures, will eat into drink time.

☐ **3am** – If by some miracle we're all still together, there's a lovely kebab shop on the corner of the strip, you can thank me after!

Day two

☐ **1pm** – (you can wake up earlier if you like, but I won't be a fully functioning adult until after 1pm, thank you)

☐ **3pm** – Boat party!!! - Can everyone wear white swimsuits? Sarah is wearing a black one, she said she will more than likely have her flowers this weekend and doesn't want to take the gamble. Can everyone send me their next of kin contacts, I am certain there will be a casualty after this.

☐ **7pm** – Stop at McDonalds for some soakage between sessions.

☐ **8pm** – Cocktail-making class in hotel bar - The fella running it is supposed to be massive!

☐ **10pm** – Karaoke bar / Drag show before we hit the clubs for one final time! Bernie, I heard you love a bit of Shania Twain!

☐ **3am** – Go to kebab shop.

Pros of such a hen party

- You'll still be talking about this weekend in twenty years' time.
- You get to have the craic with these people all over again at the wedding!
- It's abroad! Sun, pool and frozen cocktails.

Cons:

- You will need to book a week off work to recover.
- If you have young kids to go home to, I feel sorry for you.
- The unmerciful hangovers in the searing heat.
- You'll spend a fortune buying rounds of shots for your new best friends.
- You'll have to make a private story on your socials, because if the people at work saw how feral you went on this trip you'd be unemployed (and your work friends are as feral as it comes,

so that's saying something.)
- If you don't get insured, it's going to cost you a fortune, because you will *definitely* injure yourself trying to pole dance.

Excuses you can use to not attend such a hen party:
- 'I have COVID. Again.'
- Tell the maid of honour you're on antibiotics and can't drink (I'm 99 per cent certain this won't work because depending on the maid of honour, she might just say 'ah I took them tablets for me strep throat years ago and I was grand on the wine!')
- Go to the airport with a carry-on case, before you get to the security gate, say you need to use the loo and just don't come back, they'll be pissed getting off the minibus and won't notice you're gone until the flight going home. It's a lot of commitment, and those community centre acting classes you did when you were fourteen, will finally come in handy.
- Say you can't get it off work, but to be honest I'd rather go on this trip than go to work! Depending on the Maid of Honour, they might say, 'My nanny knows her doctor's receptionist very well and she can get you a sick note!'

So now that you're fully briefed on the two most common types of hen parties, you're prepared for all kinds of trials and tribulations. No matter which type of party you end up going to, it's what YOU make of it! Just pray someone else either enjoys it as much as you or is as miserable as you, and stick with them, they'll be your lifeline. Seventy-two hours isn't a lot in the grand scheme of things. However, if you're a worrier like me, this guide should prepare you for the worst!

CHAPTER 8

When Your Best Friend Becomes a Mother for the First Time

Do you remember when you and your bestie were kids, you would get insanely possessive or jealous if a new kid on the block tried to claim them? Wtf, they're *colouring* together? How long has *this* been going on! This bitch only moved onto the road ten minutes ago, who does she think she is? How could your best friend cheat on you? You refuse to share them with anyone else.

When you have a best friend, you go through plenty of ups and downs together, but they're your best friend because they can be relied on, counted on, and always available at a moment's notice for just about anything, even those emergency consult sessions via WhatsApp audios. (Can I just take a moment to mention once again, the friends who keep things brief when sending an audio message. Nobody wants a podcast to catch up on. Short and sweet, get to the point.)

Then the first boyfriend comes along, the first serious one. You know he's going to be around a while. He's one of the good ones, and she's head over heels for him. You have to bite your tongue; when you have your own man you'll expect her to be ok with you dividing time between relationship and friendship. But you look forward to her honeymoon phase fizzling out. What's the honeymoon phase? It's where you spend zero time with your bestie because she's in the love bubble with her fella. She'll eventually come out of it and soon realize she's sick of watching him play FIFA, or they've run out of things to watch on Netflix. You know things will go back to normal between the two of you.

When your friend breaks the news that she's expecting her first baby, your world comes to a screeching halt. Let's face it, even a husband is never 100 per cent permanent, but ... a child is. You're devastated, but delighted all at once; that's the best way I can describe it. You're out having lunch and ask when the best time is to book the next girls' trip and then you hear the two words, you knew one day you'd have to face, but not this soon.

SARAH

I'm pregnant. I'm about six weeks in. I took a test last night, while he waited outside the bathroom.

ENYA

You're winding me up, aren't you?

SARAH

No, I'm deadly serious. I'm pregnant, look at the test, I have it here in my bag.

ENYA

A baby? A human being?! At this age?

SARAH

Enya, I'm thirty-two!

ENYA

Would you not have got a plant first?

Reality kicks in that although you now have to share your bestie with Satan's spawn for the rest of your days together, you can't help but be overwhelmed with joy. You get to witness your best friend become a mother for the first time.

SARAH

Are you happy or not, lol?

ENYA

Of course I'm happy! Rather you than me, though.
You're still coming to Ibiza, yeah, start them young?

SARAH

I couldn't imagine anything worse.

3 Positives to your best friend being pregnant

You'll now have a lift home from the pub on a Saturday night because she can't drink, but just because she's pregnant doesn't mean she can't socialize. It's a win-win, she doesn't need a babysitter, if the baby is still inside her. (But for a limited time only, usually nine months.)

- When your bestie makes it Facebook official - This is where you put your best-friend stamp on the announcement, you run to the comment section and get your response in ASAP. 'It's finally out! It was so hard to keep this a secret the last three months. You're going to be the best mother, I can't believe my best friend is having a baby, MY BEST FRIEND!!'

- The gender-reveal party! An opportunity to get all the gang together and celebrate the fact the baby will either have a willy or a Mary. Free cake and champagne, do it the Irish way!

- You don't have any nieces or nephews or kids yourself, so you've already taken on the fun, young, single aunt role. If it's a girl, you'll be their go-to when they have boy trouble. If it's a boy, no girl will be good enough for him! And you may or may not be responsible for them learning their first curse word.

- One day you may be a mother yourself and seeing your best friend go through it first is like a free trial without the birth part. You still have your freedom, but you'll now have some-one who's been there, done that. Someone you can go to and ask for advice and not be judged.

FUTURE MATERNAL ENYA
I told her *Coco Melon* went on holiday and that's why we can't watch it for a while.

Am I a bad mother? I just can't hack looking at that bald child for another four hours today. I'll crack, and don't even get me started on Miss Rachel, I'm blaming that one on you!

SARAH

Oh, he's gone on holiday in your house? He died a long time ago in our house. I don't blame you, no judgment here. Only so many times you can listen to, 'The wheels on the bus.'

Some negatives to your best friend being pregnant.

- You're no longer the priority anymore, get used to it. Your friend won't drop everything and run for you like they once did. Now, they will drop everything and run for their kid. You're not even in the same universe as this kid when it comes to being important to your bestie.

- Planning the baby shower. You're the best friend, it's your duty. It's not your speciality, you're more of a hen party gal, not babygros and nappies. Even when she tells you, she absolutely doesn't want one, or to put financial strain on any friends for gifts. You still have to throw her one, a surprise one.

SARAH

Oh, we're going to your house for lunch?
We've never done that before, have we?

*She walks into the living room and is
greeted by friends, family and in-laws, and
the gay best friend who just wants to know
where the wine is.*

• You're not allowed to have problems. I'm being sarcastic.
(Kind of.) Never tell a pregnant, hormone-fuelled woman
that you're tired, though:

ENYA

Jesus, I'm wrecked today for some reason.

SARAH

Oh, *you're* wrecked!? Wait until you're getting sick ten times a day, can only sleep
on your right side, piss twenty times
throughout the night because the baby is
pressing on your bladder, and don't get
me started on getting up from a chair
whon you're nine months pregnant, or if

you drop something on the floor, you're never picking it back up, it's gone, good luck.

Or a new mother:

ENYA

Oh God, I'm so tired today.

SARAH

Tired? Tired from what? Do you hear this one saying she's tired when she crawled out of the bed at nine this morning. I'd love you to swap places with me. Wait until you're breastfeeding and have to wake up three times a night against your will, and just accept your faith and just stay awake from 4am. Come back to me when you're running on three hours of sleep a night. Then you'll know what poxy tiredness is.

- Fewer nights out together. When people around you start having kids, you can kiss goodbye to last-minute nights out. Babysitters need to be booked a month in advance, and because your friend is up with a newborn or infant at the crack of dawn, they only have one or two, because from what I hear, getting up with kids whilst hungover is a death sentence, it's just not worth it.

· She will bond with other expectant mothers or mothers in general and spend a lot of her time in their company, you'll feel pushed aside. But you're not pregnant and her unborn child is now her purpose, she'll be surrounded by people who she'll want advice and guidance from. You'll be there as a support capacity too except you know sweet fuck all about pregnancy. Mainly just be there so she can moan about her fella not having to go through all the carnage! Men really do have it easy, don't they?

SARAH

I'm so tired of my tits leaking.

ENYA

I can't say I know how that feels, but sometimes if I laugh too much a little bit of piss comes out, if that's any consolation?

- Get used to going to kids' parties on a Sunday - I've been around thirty-one years, and the only place time stands still is when I'm at a child's birthday party. You were out the night before; you've got a pulsing headache. You walk into the party and are met with a shrine to *Paw Patrol*, kids screaming, crying, laughing, vomiting. They're swinging from the ceiling in the local Leisureplex. And you've to endure it for the sake of friendship. The only thing you'll get out of it is a slice of jam sponge.

The Name

Deciding on a name for the unborn child is one of the most memorable debates you'll have with your friend.

SARAH

If it's a boy I'm going to call him Ethan.

ENYA

Eaten? As in I haven't eaten anything all day?

SARAH

No, as in Eet-han.

ENYA

Oh, you wouldn't call him that, is he a fictional character from one of them American teen dramas?

SARAH

If it's a girl were going to call her Ali.

ENYA

As in Diagon Alley? From Harry Potter?

SARAH

No, Just Ali. Short and sweet.

ENYA

Where was the baby conceived?

SARAH

Bit personal!?

ENYA

I've a reason why I'm asking.

SARAH

She was conceived in Azerbaijan on our honeymoon.

ENYA

Ah jaysus. A lot of people name their kids after where they were conceived, my cousin was conceived down a lane and now her name's Elaine. Imagine giving birth to an Irish baby and calling her Azerbaijan.

SARAH

Azerbajaysus sounds a better...

ENYA

I was messing.

SARAH

I wasn't.

A mother is a bit like a finger print, no two are the same

From what I've witnessed amongst my friends going through motherhood, they all raise their kids very differently.

Type 1 – By the book

Your friend is in a constant state of worry all the time about their child, even though he or she is perfectly healthy, sitting right in front of them eating bits of Lego.

ENYA

I got a milky bar in the shop for Logan. Does he like white chocolate?

LOUISE

Oh, Jesus I wouldn't give my child that, have you not read the horror stories on children's teeth decaying before they even develop?

ENYA

Ok, relax, Hun. It's a bit of milk and cocoa powder, it's not acid.
Will we bring Logan to the park? The sun is splitting the stones, it's a great day for the playground.

LOUISE

Oh great, who doesn't want to increase

the risk of their child developing mela-noma, and as for the swings? They're a breeding ground for bacteria.

Type 2 – They build their personality around being a mother

You could be in the middle of a nightclub in Benidorm, licking peach schnapps off a barman's six pack and she'll turn to you and say, with a straight face.

NICOLA

Ah, Holly loves peaches, every time we're in the supermarket, she'll ask me, Mammy, can we get the peach ice pops.

They forget they had a life before kids, now it's their only reason to exist.

Let's not forget their soppy Facebook posts on the daily.

NICOLA

I used to think fun was going out every weekend and getting pissed, now it's sit-ting in with Mark and the kids watching Disney movies and drinking hot chocolate.

Oh, shut up, Nicola, it wasn't so long ago we were in Vegas, and you were chewing a banana from stripper's boxers at a Magic Mike show. Where were Mark and the kids then? A few double vodkas into you were like 'Who's Mark?' I've got video evidence.

Type 3 – The 'go with the flow' mother

They've seen it all, they've been through the wringer, they've dealt with the near-death experiences, the colds, the flus, the tantrums, they're as chill as it comes.

CIARA

You won't let your child have a Milky Bar? My two were chewing nuts at his age! He'll be grand for fuck's sake.

You're still putting arm bands on your kids when you're at the pool? You just throw them into the water as early as possible, that's how they learn to swim.

Why wouldn't you bring your child to a playground? God forbid they socialized with other kids. Kids will get sick no matter where you bring them, it strengthens their immune system. Are you just going to put your child in a bubble for the rest of their life? Live a little.

NICOLA

Katelynn is after falling on her ankle and hitting the concrete, Ciara. Maybe bring her to the emergency room just in case.

CIARA

Ah, would you get real. The emergency room? I fell from a three-storey building when I was her age and I survived, she'll be grand. Bit of TCP and a plaster and she'll be running around in no time. It makes them worse when you panic.

SARAH

Fairly sure it's broken by the looks.

CIARA

Broken!? She better be bleedin' messing!!

Type 4 – The guilt-free mother

I thought these were an urban legend, but some mothers do per-severe when they're on a weekend trip with the girls, or on a night out. When they get the opportunity to get out, they don't even look back! Once they drop the kids off at their grandparents or leave them at home with the father, they sprint out of the house with smoke on their heels. She even prioritizes hobbies and has no shame in asking anyone to babysit, to give herself a pamper day.

BEAUTICIAN

Oh, do you not miss the kids, when you're away, I do be riddled with guilt. I can't wait to get home and squeeze them!

NATALIE

The longest holiday I had this year was a five-minute shower. I miss the peace and quiet, that's what I miss, so excuse me for enjoying myself. I'll have another Pro-secco if it's going, too.

Type 5 – The mother who measures their child's age in months.

Please can we put a stop to this. I give the biggest eyeroll when I ask how old someone's child is and they say, 'He's twenty-seven months.'

I'm a busy woman. I don't have the time to count in months. There is a monkey banging a tambourine in my head right now. Your child is two! Just say he's two! It will save you so much time and people will be less inclined to tune out of your story.

Type 6 – The sun shines out my child's arse

Their child can do no wrong, they are perfect, they don't make mistakes, they don't hit other kids, they don't tease other kids, they're a model student. Do you know what their mother is? Delusional! The child is the opposite of everything mentioned above. They're *always* in trouble, they *always* hit other kids, they're a teacher's worst nightmare.

NATALIE

Ciara, will you chastise your child, she keeps kicking my one, she's coming home every day with bruises telling me, 'Mercedes keeps hitting me.'

STACEY

Who? *My* Mercedes? My Mercedes

wouldn't hit another child. She knows
better. I raise my kids right. Are you sure
it's not your child kicking mine? Isn't she
mad into the football? Tell her the boots
are for the ball not for my young one!

While we're on the subject of friends with kids, can we speak
about the friends who are hellbent on *not* having kids. That's perfectly ok. It's the twenty-first century, we aren't raised in a society
anymore where men are the breadwinners and women stay at
home and raise children. More women are choosing not to have
kids for practical and personal reasons. They get to their thirties and their grandmother is interrogating them at Christmas
dinner.

NANNY

When are you going to get yourself a fella
and give your mother a few grandkids?
You're getting on now, aren't you thirty-two this year?

ENYA

I'm actually ok with not having any kids,
Nanny. I'm extending my adolescence to

> have more me-time. And I actually like having the luxury of being able to leave the house at a moment's notice. I'm going backpacking next month for a year, too.

Things NOT to say to your friend who doesn't want kids.
(And also, responses to expect.)

- 'I brought the kids to ice skating this weekend and we went for food afterwards. We had a great time, watching your kids making memories and enjoying life is so magical. Sorry I'm not rubbing it in too much, am I?' *No, absolutely not, don't worry, your life literally sounds terrible to me.*

- 'You don't want kids!? Who'll take care of you when you're old and grey?' *Well, I'll have a pretty decent pension, since I'm so career driven, so someone who isn't even born yet will be getting paid to wipe my arse.*

- 'Do you not like kids? I used to always think like that, but you'll love your own.' *No, I don't like kids, and I'm very confident I wouldn't like my own either.*

- 'You won't know real love until you have kids.' *Love? Is that what you tell yourself, when you're cleaning shit soup from the crack in your child's arse every morning? And I couldn't love anything more than my chubby orange cat, who is very low maintenance and just loves doing his own thing.*

- 'The world is a better place with your kids in it.' *Relax Karen, the human race isn't going anywhere. I'll let the teenagers who are having unprotected sex in parks, take one for the team. Me having or not having a child won't affect your life in any way shape or form.*

And then of course, I'll take my own advice on this one, things *not* to say to your friend who is a new mother. Although they're mesmerised by their first baby, it's also really hard mentally and physically and the last thing they need is someone rubbing their child-free life in their face, for example:

- Not inviting them places under the assumption they just can't go.

ENYA

I'd have asked you out for lunch with me and Nicola, but I thought you'd be busy with the baby.

SARAH

I would have *loved* to get out of the house for an hour, buggies have wheels for a reason.

Even if the answer is always no, you should always ask!

• Sending them Snapchats/Insta stories of your night out, when they couldn't get a babysitter.

ENYA

You're missed tonight!

SARAH

Thanks for reminding me that I couldn't go, as if I don't have enough FOMO.

Instead, don't send them anything, and play it down when they ask if the night was good.

ENYA

Average enough, you could definitely notice your absence, I'll put it that way.

• Telling them their life is over when they become pregnant

ENYA

You're still so young, you're mad having a child. I love my freedom!

209

SARAH

It's not like I planned a child in my mid-twenties.

- Instead of reminding them of what they're missing, remind them of what they're gaining.

ENYA

Look at the life you've had so far, this is just a little pitstop before you start living it up again. And If it's a boy, You're gonna be a MILF. You'll be still young enough and fit enough off on your Ibiza holidays, when your child is reared and I'll only be nursing mine. My ma always said she wished she had me younger when she was fit as a fiddle and could chase after me.

- Thinking of yourself instead of them

ENYA

You're pregnant?
So does this mean you won't be drinking on our girls' weekend away in Kilkenny?

SARAH

There will be years upon years ahead of
us for me to drink with you on another
girls' holiday, but I'm fascinated that's
the first thing that came to mind!

Instead, remind them how accommodating you and the girls will
be to make any future trips away, to be as seamless as possible for
her:

ENYA

We can plan a lovely spa day instead,
God knows you'll need it when the ankles
start to swell up.

Making them feel worse than they already feel

*Your friend's new baby is having a crying
tantrum in the local restaurant*

ENYA

Oh my God, everyone is looking at us.
Please bring him outside, the sounds
from him are demonic!

SARAH

I know, I'm mortified, I'm so sorry!

Instead, why not threaten the other judgemental onlookers:

ENYA

Do you have a poxy staring problem?
Never hear a newborn crying before?

Now, let's get back to the point of this chapter, which is your best friend becoming a mother. We've established that it's ok to feel a bit bitter at first, like you've lost your bestie or you've lost a part of her. But you also get to see a *new* part of her, one you haven't seen before. Especially if you've been friends since you could walk and talk, you know her inside out, you've seen every side there is to see. You've seen her cry, you've seen her be sick, you've seen her drunk, you've seen her angry, you've seen her dance (if that's what she likes to call it). You've seen her fall; you've seen her get back up.

But you haven't seen her as a mother. And every first-time mother needs their best friend, because crying into your fella's shoulder about your haemorrhoids isn't sexy, but into your best friend's shoulder, it's totally normal. You might even have haemorrhoids together at this particular time, your menstrual cycles have been in sync many times, so why not piles? Before a man and woman marry, they have to declare vows to each other, before they embark on the journey of marriage together in sickness and in health and all that. So here's a vow to make to your best friend before she embarks on the journey of motherhood (well it's actually more of a letter, rather than a vow, but you get what I mean.) You can send it via email, copy and paste or whatever, but I think it's more formal through WhatsApp, or maybe a drunk phone call might seem more fitting depending on your friend group.

Dearest Bestie,

The time is almost here, I can't believe you're about to become a mother! And you're going to make a great one. How am I so sure? When we were kids playing with our Baby Born, you handled that doll like it was an actual human being; remember you let it fall, and you told us all not to ring the guards because she could be taken off you? You were so gullible. We all loved to stay over at yours after a night on the town, because when we woke up on a Sunday morning, hanging out of our arses, you loved to mammy us. You would jump up and hop into your bubble Micra. Remember that car? The driver's door didn't open or close, so you'd have to get in through the passenger seat. You'd have made a shit getaway driver. You'd come back from the shop with a bag of chicken fillet rolls, cans of Coke and heaps of paracetamol. You were already showing your maternal instincts back at nineteen.

I'm sure you're aware the first few months after baby arrives won't be easy, and you're probably not going to get much sleep. It won't be like that forever, though. And we did a season in Ibiza, hun, we barely ever slept; if you can make it through that you can make it through this. But of course I'm always around after work if you need a power nap, or just ten minutes to wash yourself in the event your fella isn't around. Take care of yourself so you can take care of the baby. Tiredness is only temporary, but watching your baby grow into a child is fleeting!

Speaking of your fella, remember you loved each other so much one night, you conceived a child in Azerbaijan? Remember that type of love, because when you want to roar the head off him for being able to sleep through the cries, or not having a pair of tits to share the workload, take a step back and remember why you love that eejit so much, because he's just learning too.

It's also okay to ask for help. Remember when you'd visit your nana and ask me to babysit your Baby Born, and I managed to keep her alive until you came back? I think I can manage this one too. Juggling a baby with 'you time' work and a social life is hard enough; it takes a team of girlos not just you and your fella.

Forgive yourself, you're going to make mistakes, you're going to fuck up, you're going to have days that seem never-ending, or impossible, or make you question your ability to be a mother. You're going to not respond to my WhatsApps. I'll be fuming at first, but I'll get over it (I wish WhatsApp had a nudge button like MSN did (joke)). You can't please everyone or be perfect! Take everything in and cherish it because the days might seem long, but the years are short. Take loads of pictures and capture the memories. When a baby grows up, they're not going to remember the days that you found the toughest, they're just going to remember the days you gave them love and attention and made them smile. I just ask you, please, please don't turn into one of those mothers who fills their Facebook timeline with pictures of their kids doing the most mundane shit, or corners them at parties and has a slide show ready to go. (I trust you won't, but I'm just making sure, because as much as I love you, I will mute you across all platforms, I have no patience for it.) Or don't become one of those mothers who take part in those mammy Facebook groups. 'Is it ok to give my thirty-four-month-old Calpol?' We did not come this far in our friendship for that to be your downfall.

Anyway, as we enter this new chapter in your life, I want you to know I'm so happy for you, I'm so proud of you, I'm so lucky you chose me as your best friend and I'm so glad this baby chose you to be his or her mammy.

Side note, are you going to be using your mobile home in Wexford next weekend? Totally cool if you are, just curious.

Love

Bestie x

CHAPTER 9

The First Friend To ...

Remember when you were a kid running around the streets causing havoc? The streetlights turning on would give a signal that it was time to go home.

My mother would always say to me, 'Don't leave the road, because your bath is in ten minutes, do ya hear me?'

I was always one of those kids who left the road regardless. I'd be around the corner with my mates, playing Kick the Can and I'd hear a car skidding in the distance, not a robbed one for a change. Have you ever seen that scene in *Jurassic Park* where the Tyrannosaurus rex breaks free and the two kids in the movie are stuck in the car, and the glass of water on the dash starts to vibrate? Something is coming, and it's big. Well, that is exactly how it felt when your mother was out for blood and you were seconds from getting the arse leathered off ya. The car would pull up, and they hadn't got electric windows in the cars back in those days, you had to manually roll it, it was like she was doing the routine to Tina Turner's 'Proud Mary' – 'ROLLING!' She'd stare into my soul, stretch her arm out through the window and do that come hither gesture.

MY MA

Get in the back of that car for your bath, NOW!!

And my friend dared to say:

FRIEND

How did you fit a bath in the back of that Fiesta?

You had no bills, no responsibilities, and you had no shame in putting the hand out for Mammy and Daddy to give you pocket money. But with getting older comes greater responsibility. Your parents are pushing you out to get a job, decide on a career path, get on the road soon. You're dying to finish school so you can be old enough to go out and do what you like and have no authority figures to answer to. But we didn't know how lucky we were. I'd give anything to go back to school and not have a single utility bill to my name, not have to pay rent, health insurance, tax or a credit union loan. I'm sure there's a list of other things I'm forgetting, but if I look at my recent bank statement, I'll be swiftly reminded.

When does that transition from teenager to adult start to appear? You see it coming when you're watching your slightly older friends progress before you do and you know your youthful days are numbered.

I'll always be an advocate for schools to teach kids how to sort their taxes or buy a house. It's been eleven years since I left school and I still haven't used the Pythagorean theorem. Not once!

The first friend to drive.

The most expensive thing my mother ever bought me as a late teen was probably a school trip to Glasgow to watch Celtic play Hibernia in the Scottish league. We were a working-class family, and I had a twin brother in the same school as me. So it was double the cost of everything when it came to school. Uniforms, books, PE tracksuits, lunch money, school trips, enrolment fees etc. My brother and I had to have a game of rock-paper-scissors to decide who got to go to Scotland. My mother would beg to steal and borrow for us, but sometimes, certain things just weren't feasible – like sending both me and my brother abroad for five days a month before Christmas. So lo and behold, I got to go! Great trip! (Don't worry he got to go on the next trip. It was to a chocolate factory about 5 km from the school at Easter time. He got a bar of chocolate with his name on it. It was nearly as good as the Glasgow trip. Anyway, back to my point, I was ecstatic to go to watch a football match in another country, while my friend who turned sixteen was given a brand-new car for her birthday. Wtf? How much money did this family *have* to hand their child something that probably cost the guts of €10,000? I was still bumming €2 off my parents on a Saturday to buy a bag of chips. When your friend gets their first car, they automatically become more mature, watching them change gears, and give right of way at roundabouts just radiates independence. When you want to get from A to B as a teenager you either have to get the bus, or else ask your parents for a lift. You could get a taxi, but when you were trying to stretch €2 over Saturday and Sunday, I think it's safe to say taxis were completely out of the question.

However, I'm at the age now where I'd rather not get on public transport. I've been driving since I was twenty-five and I couldn't imagine anything worse than having to use public transport against my will. If I'm out in the city centre having drinks with friends and I leave in time for the last bus, I'm still 100 per cent getting a taxi. I'd rather ride in comfort than take the risk of catching a mystery illness off those handrails.

The world becomes a much bigger place when your friend gets a car, it's kind of like having a chauffeur; you ride around all day like a passenger princess, listening to Rihanna while they burn through fuel money. Going through the McDonalds drive-thru just because you can. Driving through different areas on the opposite side of the city to see how the other half live. Driving out to the beach. Those late-night chats, where your friend would park up is where tea was spilled! Radio off, car in neutral, hand-brake on, McFlurry in hand, and you were ready to tell all about the latest scandal. In the Fiat Punto, the worries about talking too loud in your bedroom and waking your parents are a distant memory. Now they can't overheard you talking about something very illegal! Those car chats were almost therapeutic. I got some of the best life advice sitting in the back of my friend's car; it was a safe space. Whatever was said in the back of that Fiat Punto, stayed in the back of that Fiat Punto. Ten years on she now drives a BMW 5 series and has two kids. She obviously didn't take all my life advice onboard. (Which was, *Stay childless, you're too selfish for kids.*) If you are the friend who has a car before everyone else in the group, be prepared for your mates to become hyper-dependent on you. It's all fun and games being the only one with a car until you become a taxi driver by default. The novelty of driving wears off very quickly in that case.

The first friend to turn eighteen

I think from the moment you enter secondary school and hit puberty, your main goal is to reach the grand age of eighteen and make it out alive. I always found it fascinating that one student would be the oldest in the entire year, as their birthday was in September and then you had the youngest, whose birthday was the following June. Almost a year apart! The people who turned eighteen first in school, really rubbed it to the June heads, who still had a long way to go.

'Was out in a nightclub on Saturday with my sister's friends, didn't get home till 3am, only did the science homework last night. I was hanging, sorry am I rubbing it in too much?'

I remember my graduation ceremony in 2011. When we all went out afterwards to celebrate, there was still a handful of people who still weren't legal to drink. Scarlet for them!

Positives and negatives of being the oldest in your group:

Positives: You don't have to stand outside an off license anymore and ask some strange man to go in and buy you your alcohol for park drinks.

Negatives: All of your mates now have someone they know personally to go in and get their alcohol for them. I was that friend. I'm fairly certain the staff of the local Supervalu thought I had a drinking problem. I went in at least five times in two hours buying an array of drinks each time.

Positives: You don't need your mother's permission to go on school trips. This was something I didn't anticipate when I turned eighteen. I was still in school and when we we're going on day trips or overnight stays, I didn't have to get my mother to sign a permission slip. I was an adult now in charge of my own self. It felt liberating.

TEACHER

Ok, guys, remember you can't go on your trip tomorrow unless I get all permission signed and handed back to me. Enya you're ok, you're eighteen.

ENYA

Yes. Yes, I am!

The buzzkill was that you couldn't write yourself sick notes or give yourself a note to get off early. They didn't give you *total* liberty.

Negatives: But of course having an Irish mother, it didn't mean jack shit. As much as I fantasized about not having anyone to answer to about my weekend antics once I was of legal age, I was humbled very quickly, since I still lived at home and still relied on my parents for pocket money.

Sunday 3am. Enya bursts through the front door.

MA

What time do you call this! I've been worried sick!

ENYA

I was out with my friends drinking, I'm eighteen now and I should be able to do what I want!

MA

Not when you're living under this roof, because when you are, you're living

> under my rules! Don't forget who funds
> your nights out! We wouldn't want that to
> come to a stop, would we?

The first friend to share a house with you.

All I ever wanted to do was live with my best friends when I was a kid. I would hate going home to sit in my room all by myself. On a high all day of riding our bikes, colouring, playing games only to stare at four walls once it was bedtime, there were no social media platforms or messaging apps back then. Remember phoning your friend on the house phone and having to speak to their parents directly? Whenever my friend was grounded for a long period, I wouldn't hear from her at all; she could have been dead for all I knew! I'd either have to wait for a knock on my door one day or wait on a phone call to tell me she's on temporary release. I wanted to be around my friends all the time!

However, they do say, 'if you want to know me come live with me'. That statement is true indeed, not just in relationships but with friendships too. You thought it was going to be all rainbows moving in with your friend for the first time, you had high hopes. Parties, movie nights, and so on, but you were sorely mistaken. Maybe seeing your friend in small doses was what kept the friendship alive. The first few months are great, you're in the honeymoon period of having your own place together. No parents to answer to, nobody nagging about cleaning up, YET. Being able to come and go as you please and bringing boys back on the weekend and not having to sneak them out the following morning.

Then reality sets in. Your protein yoghurts start disappearing from the fridge, the dishwasher hasn't been emptied when you were told it would be, tea bags thrown in the sink. Tampons blocking the loo. Work friends being brought home at all hours on the weekend. And they're just *your* bad habits! It's not long before you butt heads and realize that you *thought* living together would be amazing, but you were looking at it through rose-tinted glasses. Living with a stranger is more sustainable as you're not using the person you knew the last twenty years as a reference versus the person they really are once you live with them. To salvage the friendship you're best living separately as absence does make the heart grow fonder.

The first friend to come out of the closet.

I believe in something called the 'gay best friend distribution system'. Every girl needs a gay friend in her life. They will find you, and you'll be friends for life. Usually, you'll stumble across them in your council estate or in school, or even in the workplace. Living a long and healthy life is only enhanced by befriending someone from the LGBTQ+ community. If you meet them early on, in childhood, it won't make sense to you at first, but as you grow into your teens, you'll start to pick up on comments they make about boys or girls, or how they dress or their mannerisms, or their obsession with *America's Next Top Model* and also Madonna. You'll never confront them to confirm your suspicions, because it's their life and their business. You'll support them and love them no matter what. Their sexual orientation won't impact any part of your friendship. The day will come, however, when they will state the obvious. The fact they want to tell you and not just have you assume it, is because they trust you and love you. It will also be in the most nonchalant manner too. You'll probably be on a drive somewhere in that Fiat Punto I mentioned earlier.

SARAH

Anyone any goss to share.

GAY FRIEND

No, not really, other than I'm gay.

COLLECTIVELY

We know. We knew before you even knew.

GAY FRIEND

Cool, who wants to get McNuggets with me?

If you weren't blessed with a gay friend as a child, there's still time for them to enter your life as an adult. And they'll enter your life in the most flamboyant way possible, by being completely blunt at a friend's birthday party.

GAY FRIEND

Heya, I'm Derek, I'm Martina's friend, and can I just say, I'm loving the hair, but the make-up, just no. Like something from the Wrong Turn. I know you can do better. I'm a MUA and I'll do you any-time, trust me you'll thank me when all the fellas want to ride you once I'm done with ya.

ENYA

Thanks, I think?

What are the benefits to having a gay friend in your life?

- They're brutally honest! (Refer to the scenario above.) A gay best friend will be your biggest supporter but also won't blow smoke up your arse. While all your girls try to convince you that your dress is fab, your gay guy best friend is the first to call bullshit.

- They've got a great sense of fashion. The way a make-up artist remembers a face and what cosmetics make it look its best, your gay friend will only let you wear something that show-cases all the right curves in all the right places.

GAY FRIEND

No, you are not coming to the same bar as me dressed like Kathy Bates. Green is *definitely* not your colour, nor are skater skirts for you! Get back in there and change and don't come back out until you find that black dress you wore to my thirtieth, that was fab on you – it gave you a great arse.

- The only man you'll fart around. As much as we love our part-ners or spouses, there's always a tiny bit of us that's reserved for friends only. And if you're a gay man, you get the VIP experience, she is definitely not hiding any of her true self from you. Just like when you go on a girls' trip and your gay pal is lying on the bed scrolling through TikTok and you walk out from the shower in the nip, baring all, asking where your moisturizer is, and he says:

GAY FRIEND

Ew, put a towel on, ya gowl.

You know you have nothing to worry about.

- They are a fountain of knowledge when it comes to pop culture, specifically Kylie Minogue and Britney Spears and also (strangely?) Princess Diana. One of my gay besties has a photo of her on her nightstand, wtf? They are a walking encyclopaedia when it comes to the Gen Z queens. So if you ever need to know why a celeb marriage broke up or why Kim Kardashian won't be returning for a fifth season, your gay best friend will know before the papers do.

- Lastly, they are naturally gifted comedians. I don't know how and I don't know why, but they have a way with words like no other friend. Their comic relief is always warranted in any situation. I could list many one-liners my own gay friend has said in the past, but it would be *a have to be there moment* for you to roll around laughing. Let's just say they help me with a lot of my stand-up material without ever knowing. And if I ever did NOT want someone to roast me at my own wedding it would be them. I would retire from comedy because it would not be able to be topped.

The First Friend to Get Married

Even if you never get married, being a part of the most important day of your friend's life is magical. But it reminds me of Christmas Day; although the day itself is a lovely wholesome day with your friends and family, it's the build up to Christmas that is the best part. Likewise with a wedding day. Being told you're a maid of honour or a bridesmaid is like a full-circle moment because you still remember like it was yesterday sitting in her bedroom, plaiting each other's hair, watching the Disney channel, talking about your wedding day in years to come and making a promise that no matter what, you'll be standing at the altar with each other. The hen party is probably the best part of any friend getting married because you get to carry on disgracefully away from the watchful eye of the *judgies*! You get it out of your system so you can behave in an appropriate manner come the big day.

What you're not prepared for is the organization that goes into planning a wedding and also, the financial stress! Holy shit. It's not until you're involved so closely with one that you realize how much these things cost. Which is why a lot of married couples say, 'In hindsight, we should have just eloped.'

GAY FRIEND
€150 a head for a meal!?

BRIDE

Yeah, that's the going rate for a four-star
hotel.

GAY FRIEND

Is the cow made of gold or what?

Also, bridezilla is a real thing, because it's the law that when
one thing goes wrong weeks before the wedding, e.g. the photographer drops dead, you can guarantee three or four more things
will go wrong also, and the poor groom will get the brunt of it,
because the WhatsApp group becomes a sound board for how
he hasn't a clue about table centrepieces or seating arrangements.

BRIDE

The photographer cancelled and Tomo
suggested we just get everyone to take
pictures on their phones, he said his
Samsung 25 Ultra is bleedin' deadly.

MAID OF HONOUR

Oh, for fuck's sake. That's men for ya.

BRIDE

I said, are you for real? It's our wedding day?

And then he said, well we will buy a disposable camera as well then! I'm fuming, girls, I'm actually fuming.

BRIDESMAID

He hasn't a fucking clue!

My uncle is a forensic photographer. He's free the weekend of the wedding if you want me to ask him to do it.

BRIDE

Is that a joke?

BRIDESMAID

No?

BRIDE

Thanks, Hun, but I want to be upright in my photos, not faceplanting the floor with chalk drawn around me.

*This is where your maid of honour duties
kick in. It's time to step up.*

MAID OF HONOUR

I made a few phone calls, the girl who did
my sister-in-law's wedding. She'll cancel
a corporate gig to do it. Same price too.

BRIDE

How did you pull that one off?

MAID OF HONOUR

I had to sell my Coldplay tickets.

The eve of the wedding is a special moment in a friendship, you'll
gather around the island in the kitchen, it's 1am, you're a few Pro-
seccos deep and reminiscing about old times. Before boys, before
life, before you grew up. Until it dawns on you, the first friend of
the group is about to sign her life away to a man.

MAID OF HONOUR

I can't believe you're going to have a husband after tomorrow! Wtf!?

BRIDESMAID

I can't believe I managed to still fit into
my dress.

GAY FRIEND

I can't believe you're gonna have to ride
the same fella for the rest of your life!

The wedding day arrives, you get the hair and make-up done, put the gowns on and watch your best friend marry the love of her life. Is it even a wedding ceremony unless somebody is appointed to press play on Spotify for the bride's entrance and before the song starts, you hear 'THE BLUETOOTH DEVICE IS READY TO PAIR.' After spending 70k on the wedding you couldn't even get the local karaoke champion to sing Shania Twain's *From this Moment*.

The Maid of Honour is also in charge of the cards. You or the best man, but let's be honest, you'll be more responsible than him. That means when the happy couple are looking to pay the band, you've got to rip them all open up in their suite and gather the cash together.

The wedding speeches.

If you're a maid of honour or a bridesmaid, I hope you don't fear public speaking, because unfortunately this is mandatory. As a comic, I'll give the future Maids of Honour a few pointers. Always open with a joke: 'I'm so happy to have organized these next ten minutes, the only ten minutes that the bride and groom didn't get to organize' or if you want to play it cocky. 'Hi, everyone, I'm the Maid of Honour. Before I start my speech, just a few housekeeping rules the venue has asked me to ask if you could refrain from getting up on the chairs and tables, for my standing ovation after this speech. It would be much appreciated, thanks.'

Things to mention in the speech:

How you and the bride know each other: talk about when she first met the groom and exaggerate what she really thought of him, reveal some funny things the groom maybe doesn't know about her past, but that won't jeopardize her marriage! Or remember that one incident your best friend swore you to never speak about to anyone because she'd be absolutely mortified? Bring that up. What's she going to do? Take the mic off you? No chance. Don't mention ex boyfriends. And For the closing toast – threaten the groom.

MAID OF HONOUR

And before we raise a toast, I'd just like

to thank the groom for making my best
friend so happy, and also if you ever hurt
her, I'll hang your balls from me Christmas tree, cheers to the happy couple!

In Conclusion ...

I'd like to make my own toast! I hope this book has made you appreciate your friends that little bit more. Sometimes we just need a brief reminder of how much of an impact friendship has on the course of our lives. Friends help shape our identity. Friendship is a cornerstone of a woman's life, enriching her experiences, carrying her through challenges and uplifting her in moments of joy. From providing a safe space for vulnerability to offering waves of support, the craic and personal growth, a friendship is an invaluable asset that enhances every aspect of a woman's journey.

I'd like to speak on behalf of anyone who has a really good friend in their life – past, present and the ones who are due to arrive down the line. I am overwhelmed with gratitude for your presence in my life. Through every high and low, you've been there. Steady in your support, understanding and love. And it's writing (or reading!) a book like this that's reminded of how incredibly lucky I am to have you.

They say that friends are the family we get to choose, and I couldn't agree more. While our paths may not have crossed through blood, the bond we share is just as strong, if not stronger. We've laughed together until our stomachs hurt, wiped each other's tears during times of sorrow, and celebrated each other's victories as if they were our own. In every sense of the word, my friends have been my rocks, my confidants, and my partners in crime.

What makes our friendship so special is the freedom to be ourselves without judgment. With friends, I can let down my guard, share my deepest fears and wildest dreams, and know that they'll always be there to listen, support, and uplift me. It's a rare and beautiful thing to find someone who accepts you whole-heartedly, flaws and all, and I'm endlessly grateful to have found that in my friends.

But what truly defines our friendship is the choice we make, every day, to show up for each other. Whether it's a late-night phone call to talk through problems, a surprise visit just to say 'hello', or a simple text to check in, we consistently choose to prioritize each other's happiness and well-being. In a world that can often feel chaotic and uncertain, having someone like that by my side makes all the difference.

So, my dear friends, as I reflect on the countless memories we've shared and the countless more that lie ahead, I want you to know just how much you mean to me. You've filled my life with laughter, and love, and I'm absolutely raging we won't be able to attend each other's funeral, as morbid as it sounds. I am endlessly grateful for the gift of your friendship. Thank you for being the family I've chosen, and for making every moment we spend together truly special.

If you have a special friend near or abroad, give them a bell, they might need it more than you think.

With all my love and appreciation,

Enya x